LIGHTS, CAMERA, MAGIC!
THE MAKING OF

FANTASTIC BEASTS
THE CRIMES OF GRINDELWALD™

IAN NATHAN

HARPER
DESIGN
An Imprint of HarperCollins Publishers

CONTENTS

FONDE
EN 1790

FOREWORD

I've had great scripts that ended up being shoddy films and dodgy scripts that end up being great films. All you can go on as an actor is an instinct, and when I read *Fantastic Beasts and Where to Find Them*, I remember coming to the very end, when Queenie and Jacob part, and being profoundly moved by it. When I watched *Fantastic Beasts* for the first time and Dan and Alison said goodbye in the Obliviating rain, I was in pieces. It was one of those rare occasions where the script and the film making process met each other head to head.

So, it has been a true joy to get the band back together and to return to this world and explore these characters once more.

What's unique for us on these films is that many of the characters don't originate in books. They are purely born out of J.K. Rowling's imagination, and with that comes a wee bit of responsibility. Jo, of course, has one of the finest imaginations in the world, and you want to flesh out, and do justice to those characters and show her all the colours that she has dreamt up. But what is amazing about Jo is that while she has such an intricate knowledge of who her characters are, she also encourages you to really delve under the skin of these people.

Whether it's David Yates, our leader; Stuart Craig, the production designer; or Colleen Atwood, the costume designer; right down to the intricacies of the visual effects and creature design, every single department is being encouraged to push their imaginations to the limit, and it's the collective of that which makes it so unique.

Returning for *The Crimes of Grindelwald* has been like returning to school.

Those friendships at the core of the first film were replicated through our making of these films. I adore Katherine, Dan and Alison. They are all such unique and brilliant people and it's a true treat to be on this journey with them as our characters change, grow and things get a whole lot darker!

If the tone of the first film felt like an adventure, this is a thriller. It's taking these characters that you've met, this quartet of misfit heroes, and embedding them back into the Potter lore that we all know and love — the histories that were hinted at in the first film are really being opened up and explored, and with that the stakes get higher. There is a new threat as Grindelwald mobilizes and that brings a tonal difference. You still have the creatures. You still have the exasperating but heavenly Nifflers. You still have Jacob and Newt's sort of buddy romance. That lightness remains, but there's a steeliness to our new story.

It is definitely taking Newt somewhere new.

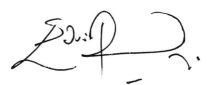

Newt signs copies of his book at Flourish & Blotts.

ESCAPE *from* NEW YORK

GRINDELWALD'S GREAT ESCAPE

On the rooftop of MACUSA, a high-security carriage waits to transport Grindelwald back to Europe to stand trial for his crimes. It is as black and uninviting as a hearse, with a team of (computer-generated) Thestrals — the opaque, skeletal horses, with bat-like wings and forbidding, dragonish snouts first seen in *Harry Potter and the Order of the Phoenix.* No one seems to be paying any regard to the fact that Thestrals are known to be auguries of misfortune.

Still, given Apparition doesn't work over long distances — certainly not across the Atlantic Ocean — they need to use a flying coach. A party of MACUSA Aurors, including Abernathy, Madam Picquery and the German wizard Spielman, Head of Incarceration at the International Confederation of Wizards, have come to retrieve their captive.

We first find Johnny Depp's notorious Grindelwald held fast to a chair in one of the stark cells in the roots of the skyscraper. While in reality his incarceration has not been lengthy, coated as he is in dust, barely stirring, it looks as if he has been sat there for centuries. His hair has grown long and lank. An unkempt beard covers his chin. Only the air around him shimmers, charged with protective spells.

'We had some of the original set from the first film, but Grindelwald's metal cell is entirely new,' says Paul Hayes, the film's construction manager. What began as one or two cells, swiftly

CASE NO.

935-470/7

M.A.C.U.S.A - F.B.C.V.N.O No. 935

VALIDATED BY

[signature]

M.A.C.U.S.A. REGISTERED OFFICE №280205

Concept art of the Thestral-drawn flying carriage leaving MACUSA by Eva Kuntz.

expanded into a row of fifteen lockups done in a compressed, abstract style, with a staircase and elevator that emerges onto the MACUSA rooftop.

'We didn't get involved with the rooftop before now,' says production designer Stuart Craig, 'but it was always part of the appeal for Jo that the uppermost level of the Woolworth Building was in the Gothic style, although it is a modern skyscraper.'

Gothic design, Craig points out, is synonymous with the wizarding world — Hogwarts being the prime example.

The new set was to represent a big open area at the top of MACUSA, so Craig returned to the Woolworth Building to specifically photograph those Gothic accoutrements and landings at its summit, and collect scale drawings of the layout, in order to faithfully reproduce the real thing on the backlot at Warner Bros. Studios Leavesden.

'We've taken licence, of course,' he explains, 'we've had to clear sufficient space to allow for a carriage and Thestrals, which is a long piece of equipment.'

Different versions of the carriage were made in Poland by a team of specialists, in the classical, eighteenth-century coach design that give a touch of European antiquity to the gleaming metropolis. The primary, 'hero' version of the carriage was for establishing shots of the rooftop. The second, says Craig, was 'cut and carved' to facilitate the ensuing stuntwork and special effects requirements.

While still on the roof of MACUSA, an elaborate crest can be seen on the carriage door, care of the industrious graphic design partnership of Miraphora Mina and Eduardo Lima, whose work requires a detailed consideration of backstory.

'We were trying to figure out who this carriage belongs to,' says Mina. 'Who is taking Grindelwald back [to Europe]?' asks Lima.

'We found that Jo had written about an International Confederation of Wizards,' continues Mina. 'So we did a monogram for them.'

Inside the carriage, Pierre Bohanna's special props department provided a set of decorative lamps, as well as an elaborate sequence of mechanical locks.

Above: New York Ghost headline announces Grindelwald's extradition date is confirmed. *Left:* Gellert Grindelwald: the prisoner of MACUSA.

'It's to give visual effects a scene where the carriage locks down,' he says. 'I'd seen this engineering process where they are able to cut fine fretwork out of thick steel. Even steel plate. So forms can lift out of the sheet metal like sculpture. Stuart loved it.'

What began merely as an extension of the door lock became an entire panel on the outside of the carriage containing an orchestra of interconnected locks.

Spielman will accompany Grindelwald, with a team of Aurors forming an escort on broomsticks. He also takes possession of a beautiful box, supposedly containing the Elder Wand and a vial holding a mysterious substance. All is not what it seems, however, and high above New York and then out over the Atlantic a thrilling mid-air escape sequence begins.

For one thing, inside the wand box is a Chupacabra: a blood-sucking beast, which takes a sizeable chunk out of Spielman, who is then cast out of the carriage.

'The whole sequence was a very complicated crossover between departments — visual effects and the art department especially,' says set decorator Anna Pinnock.

The stunt department were in their element, climbing over the carriage, hanging onto the axles and suspension underneath, and zipping about on brooms.

'Quite a fight takes place as the carriage flies across the world,' says Craig. 'So special effects had a big requirement to make the carriage move and bounce in a credible way. Stuntmen had to work out how they would climb over it and under it, in it and out of it.'

The whole thing took five months of planning and storyboarding before several weeks of shooting against a green screen. 'We were trying out different ideas,' says visual effects supervisor Christian Manz. 'As we've got a flying carriage, this was a great opportunity to introduce broomsticks back into the world, because that was something that

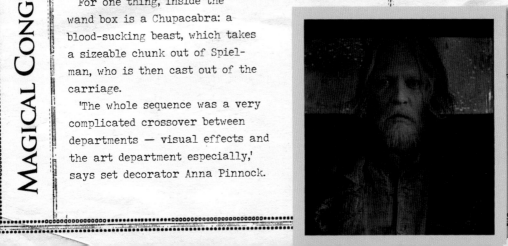

Above: Concept art of MACUSA's top floor by Eva Kuntz. *Left:* After his imprisonment, Grindelwald appears dishevelled but still full of menace.

we hadn't done with adults much in the Potter world.'

That said, the physical rig they have designed for the broomstick sequences is far more sophisticated and, hopefully, realistic than anything used on previous films.

'We're shooting it for real,' says Manz, meaning with real stuntmen on brooms not digital doubles. 'We are able to actually get broom riders right next to the carriage.'

'We've seen broomstick riding really develop over the years,' adds Tolga Kenan, the onetime gymnast who served as Daniel Radcliffe's broomstick double from the age of ten. 'It's very different now. It's a lot more wire based. We've got these things called tuning forks, which we fly the performers on.'

Bohanna's department has been largely responsible for the upgrade in broom technology (chronology notwithstanding), and he is justly proud that, rather than the convenience of computer-generated effects there are now genuine actors piloting purpose-built brooms outfitted with some cool new stirrups.

'We have developed a new, more dynamic way of mounting controlled brooms,' he says, referring to the aforementioned 'tuning forks'. 'We were very pleased how this has moved on. It's not a visual effect. It's all physical, in-camera stuff. But they were able to be much more dynamic with it.

CONFISCATED ITEM – LEVEL 9

(In accordance with MACUSA INVESTIGATION DEPARTMENT (MID) terms of conduct and by law No. 3748/274. Definitions of articles can be reviewed by application (by owl) to MACUSA chief of staff, stating code 84/1.

CONFISCATED ITEM: WAND

NAME OF OFFENDER: GELLERT GRINDELWALD

GRADES OF VIOLATION

1 2 3 4 5 6 7 8 (9) X

CASE NO.

935 - 470/7

MACUSA - F.B.C.V.R.O No. 935

Essentially we are flying the person rather than flying the broom. The broom is more lightweight and it's carried on the harnesses that the guys wear underneath their costume. It's looking really good.'

'It's all about the storytelling,' concludes Manz. 'You've got this real pursuit, a classic chase sequence with Abernathy and Grindelwald both inside and outside the carriage. We've got the carriage filling up with water and people nearly drowning inside it. It travels from the top of MACUSA across New York, down across the Hudson River and out across the sea. It's been fun to try and come up with something new and exciting.'

Finally, when Grindelwald takes control of the hijacked carriage, the opening credits roll. The film is only getting started...

Concept art of Grindelwald in a MACUSA cell by Molly Sole.

LONDON CALLING

RECREATING PERIOD LONDON

THE FOGBOUND STREETS

As Newt retreats homewards from the Ministry of Magic, wending his way through the glum London afternoon, the wizard feels a tap on his shoulder from a disembodied leather glove...

When it came to creating the streets of London of 1927 — as with Paris to come — the key was to conjure up a suitably moody atmosphere. This was, after all, to be a thriller.

Production designer Stuart Craig and his team researched a lot of 'old British movies', including the rich vein of Ealing comedies. 'London was always portrayed as foggy,' he says, 'and it became this jokey cliché in a way — this idea of London having this permanent murky atmosphere.'

One of the chief delights of working in the Wizarding World is the chance to put a magical spin on such movie clichés.

'It seemed a good thing to revive that tradition,' continues Craig, 'and we have a long sequence with Newt walking through an old-fashioned foggy London. It is rather beautifully done, the way layers of background are filtered, and you get this aerial perspective looking off into the misty distance.'

Fog has the added advantage of desaturating the colours to achieve what the designer refers to as 'an expressionist, film noir look.' Out of this misty veneer loom famous landmarks such as Lambeth Bridge, Victoria Station, and Trafalgar Square.

'Once we get to Paris,' adds Craig, 'there is a sequence in the sewers very reminiscent of *The Third Man*.'

Three views of London by concept artist Eva Kuntz.

A SECRET MEETiNG

When Newt clasps the floating glove in a hand-shake he instantly Disapparates and arrives on top of the iconic dome of St Paul's Cathedral. There stands Dumbledore, decades younger than the grey-haired headmaster we know so well, wearing the other glove.

Understandably, the summit of the 360-foot cathedral was deemed out of bounds for A-list stars. Nevertheless, in order to build an accurate replica on the backlot, Craig and his team were given access to the roof to shoot background plates. 'There was one particular statue of a seated figure high up that we copied,' he recalls, as well as the parapets for Newt and Dumbledore to walk and talk.

'It's very typical of what we do,' says Craig, 'we built a big chunk of foreground set physically and put a green screen at the end of it. Then visual effects seamlessly add the background.'

Newt and Dumbledore will finish their plotting at street level, with the background plate shot early one Sunday morning on location.

'There is a very good street behind the Bank of England,' says Craig. 'It is strong architecturally, but it does have a few traffic signs.'

Redressing a modern London street to pass as 1927 is the province of the graphic design team. 'It's funny all the lengths you have to go to,' says Miraphora Mina. 'Our assistants, poor things, had to figure out exactly what number to put on the passing bus. We needed to figure out what routes actually ran in 1927. Otherwise you get it in the neck. If you're going to put a number on there, it's better not to put the one that's going through, say, Chiswick.'

Moreover, every panel on the bus required the appropriate, time-specific advertising, including all the staircase frames on the interior of the old double-decker.

Then there was the correct style of street sign, which means working out exactly which streets their path will supposedly cross. Mina says, 'You're creating a kind of fiction upon fiction because the view through the street was of

Artificial smoke in the huge sound-stage recreates the fogbound streets of London for Eddie Redmayne and Jude Law.

St Paul's, so there's only one or two streets that that could be. But then that didn't suit the crossroads you saw earlier... It's trying to manipulate the reality with what suits best.'

Finally, the visual effects department eliminates any further trace of the modern world, including the white and yellow lines on the road. 'They look so modern,' explains Craig, 'the yellow ones particularly are non-period.'

Only then can they move onto the *next* street.

A BACHELOR PAD

His conversation with Dumbledore concluded, Newt at last returns home across Lambeth Bridge, with Parliament's iconic outline in the background.

'It is actually quite a long journey,' says Craig, and one that might be tricky to follow in real-life. 'We didn't ever actually draw a map of this composite world, with a bit of St Paul's, a bit of the Bank of England, a bit of Lambeth. We've cheated a little bit, but in a way that adds up to an interesting journey.'

According to Craig, Newt's Georgian terraced apartment is to be found in 'one of those houses with a lot of stucco on the facades so typical of London.'

Given this was 1927, they added a layer of soot to the spotless exterior of the building. 'This was long before the Clean Air Act in the sixties, due to industrial pollution creating sootiness on buildings,' explains Craig. 'This was particularly apparent in London, because so much of London is white Portland stone. It is a very important element both in Paris and London: this industrial pollution, all these black stains. It is an interesting look.'

Not only does it add to their moody film noir sensibility, it has a metaphorical sense as well. There is a darkness rising in the world, seeping into the very stone.

Inside, the decoration is strikingly mundane.

'We decided that Newt would really live in his basement, so upstairs it was furnished as sparsely as possible,' explains set decorator Anna Pinnock. What few loving touches there are have been provided by Bunty, Newt's assistant, housekeeper and secret admirer. Sadly, such touches go largely

ignored by an oblivious Newt. This is mostly the spartan décor of a mind focused elsewhere.

The graphic design team's quota ran to little more than magically branded biscuits and other sundry goods. 'There were a few products, because Newt ends up cooking dinner for Jacob and Queenie here,' recalls Eduardo Lima, 'but nothing else.'

There was a discussion as to whether Newt even slept in this stark environment. 'He probably doesn't,' concludes Eddie Redmayne. 'He sleeps down in his basement.'

As you may have gathered, it is Newt's basement, accessed via an unassuming closet door, where things get a whole lot more interesting.

A rare foray on to the real streets of London as the crew film behind the Bank of England *(top)*, and back on set as Jude Law and Eddie Redmayne stand between full-size props of period buses *(above)*.

DAVID YATES – DIRECTOR

Between takes on the second of what is set to be a quintet of *Fantastic Beasts* adventures, David Yates takes a moment to consider what he enjoys so much about the Wizarding World. After all, this might be his sixth turn behind the camera among the lavish trappings of witchcraft and wizardry, but it still feels as exciting as the first. Which, for the record, was *Harry Potter and the Order of the Phoenix*.

'What I like about Jo Rowling as a writer is even though it's a consistent universe with lots of rules and ideas that she's very carefully worked out, every time I come to make something of hers, it's always slightly different than it was before. The first *Fantastic Beasts* was a very whimsical, beautiful story of these four goofy outsiders — almost kids channelled into adults — who get dragged into a much darker, dangerous, more compelling story. Which was quite different from Harry Potter.'

In other words, when you're dealing with Rowling's apparently bottomless imagination it just never gets old. Unless, that is, it's supposed to get old. In this case: New York, London, Paris and Hogwarts in the late twenties, and, fascinatingly, a return to the famous School of Witchcraft and Wizardry from a decade earlier. All written with the panache and pace of an espionage thriller.

David Yates directs Hogwarts students in the Defence Against the Dark Arts classroom.

'When Jo sent me the first draft of *Beasts 2*, again it felt very different,' says Yates. 'It's more layered. It's more complex. There's more going on. There are more character strands developing.'

Set in motion by Grindelwald's dramatic mid-air escape from MACUSA, events will swoop back over the Atlantic. As Grindelwald's machinations take shape, Newt, Tina, Queenie and Jacob will converge on Paris, with the location of runaway Obscurial Credence still of the utmost importance. Here they will encounter the Ministère des Affaires Magiques de la France, the ramshackle Circus Arcanus, and the house of Nicolas Flamel, locked in time, where a near-immortal wizard dabbles in alchemy. Along the way, we will stop by London, see Newt's apartment, and more importantly his extraordinary basement. We will also return to Hogwarts and meet a young Dumbledore. Other new characters include Newt's charming older brother Theseus and school friend Leta Lestrange, and the mysterious Maledictus.

Yates really feels Rowling has hit her stride in terms of filmmaking. 'Which is a very different form to novel writing,' he points out. 'She was learning to walk on the last one. Now, she's picking up a sprint.'

After happily giving five years of his life to the final four Harry Potter films, Yates was convinced his time in the Wizarding World was done. Hadn't Rowling promised there would be no more books? With his grounding in high-end television drama (the humanity he instilled into the acclaimed thrillers *State of Play* and *Sex Traffic* was the reason producer David Heyman had first offered him Harry Potter), he yearned for new horizons. Life after Hogwarts began with the pilot for the television drama *Tyrant*, set in the Middle East, and was soon followed by an epic reimagining of Edgar Rice Burroughs's vine-swinging hero in *The Legend of Tarzan*, with Alexander Skarsgård and Margot Robbie. He had been planning a biopic of Al Capone.

That was before Heyman called with a secret to tell. Rowling had written an original script set decades before Harry Potter, but contained in the same universe. It concerned an unusual Magizoologist named Newt Scamander.

Yates couldn't resist taking a peek. He should have known better. It was like some kind of spell — don't open the box marked 'J.K. Rowling'. He was hooked from the opening page, desperate to direct. Capone and whatever other opportunities there might be were vastly outweighed by

Directing Eddie Redmayne for a scene in London.

Leta Lestrange, William Nadylam as the mysterious Yusuf Kama, Brontis Jodorowsky as 600-year-old alchemist Nicolas Flamel, and Johnny Depp revealing all of Grindelwald's seductive deceptions.

'There's the real underbelly of a thriller,' agrees producer David Heyman, who has developed such an easy shorthand with Yates, 'but at the same time, it's funny. There is human comedy, and also absurd humour at times. I love that Jo's writing is so multicoloured.'

As with all of the stories in Rowling's Wizarding World, as well as its share of secrets and twists, the new film is layered with themes. 'It's about truths and half-truths, and it's about identity,' says Heyman. 'It's about Grindelwald, the search for Credence, and Credence's own search for who he is. It's about the yearning and longing for love, and all that stands in the way of that. And it's this thirties film noir-style thriller like The Third Man.'

Grindelwald's drive for purity within the wizarding world parallels the rise of fascism in the early part of the twentieth century. Both director and producer recognize the film also speaks to the cruelties of our own time as much as the past.

And lest we forget, it is still a film about beasts — fantastic beasts.

'We've got a wonderful character called the Maledictus,' says Yates. 'She's slowly turning into a snake, and wants to be a woman while she still can. There is a really beautiful story of how she tries to cling onto her humanity.'

There is also a Zouwu, a Chinese beast that can run a thousand miles in a single day. 'We're exploring how it can shift through space and time,' says Yates, 'it's quite big. We've got some amazing cats called Matagots.'

These feline guardians patrol the many chambers of the French ministry keeping a sharp eye out for uninvited wizards.

the adventure that lay ahead.

Returning for the second, he says, has come with numerous pleasures. 'First of all, there was the thrill of getting reacquainted with old friends. I formed an attachment to those characters as well as the actors. You build a good relationship with the people and the minute they walk into the movie, you go, "Newt is back," only he's in a very different situation.'

Then there is the excitement of getting to grips with new characters and new actors to fill their shoes: Callum Turner as Theseus, Zoë Kravitz as

The basement of Newt's London flat provides a veritable menagerie of beasts in need of some TLC from the Magizoologist: A Kelpie, Mooncalves, Bowtruckles, baby Nifflers, and an Augurey. Newt's devotion signals another of Fantastic Beasts' great themes — environmental conservation.

'Apart from the symbolic connotations of the beastly world and the beasts within us, I think that people with modern sensibilities will view Newt's approach to these creatures as entirely ordinary,' explains Rowling. 'But the world hasn't always been like that and actually in some parts of the world right now, obviously, that is not the view that people take. So that's at the core of Newt as a character. He's actually defying the wizarding law of the time to save some of these creatures.'

Indeed, the new film introduces the evil Grimmson, a beast hunter. The director thinks of him as 'Newt's dark twin': 'Newt wants the world to understand these extraordinary creatures. Grimmson tracks them down and kills them.'

For both Yates and Heyman, it is impossible to conceive of making these films without the incredible, award-winning team they have established behind the camera. It might be a cliché, but it really feels like an extended family. All the department heads — not least: director of photography Philippe Rousselot, production designer Stuart Craig, set decorator Anna Pinnock, costume designer Colleen Atwood and visual effects supervisors Tim Burke and Christian Manz, whose department brings the magical beasts to life — worked on the first film. Indeed, many of them go back to the Harry Potter films. Craig has been designing this world for eighteen years, and is largely responsible for defining the aesthetic of the cinematic wizarding world. There is a trust and fluency between the various elements of production, and a determination to outdo what has come before.

These films remain a true collaboration, where the final say lies with Yates, from a filmmaking perspective, and Rowling, from a world-building perspective.

Every member of the cast speaks of the care and attention their director brings to the set. He is untroubled by the trademark furies of a movie director, yet still steers this massive ship with conviction. The numerous demands on his time made by the huge logistical challenge of making a multi-million-dollar film loaded with special effects notwithstanding, Yates spends time on the performances — and not allowing his actors to get too comfortable.

'He'll call you out if he needs to,' notes Dan Fogler. 'He'll give you the most gentle but blunt direction that is perfect and precise in the moment. He gets the most amazing performance out of me. He's always, "I love it, I love it. It's fab. Do it again!"'

'What I love about what he's done with this film,' says Eddie Redmayne, 'is that he has reacted to how Jo has shifted the whole infrastructure into such a different place. It's less pre-ordained, he's thinking on his feet. He is one of the most kindhearted people, but he has made sure we never feel settled or safe, because these characters are being pushed into corners. There is a vibrancy to what we are doing.'

'Yet there's always the bigger picture,' says Jude Law: 'the huge technical input into how it's filmed, and on top of that what's going to be added digitally afterwards, whether it's creatures or backdrops or the magic to be conjured. And he does it just effortlessly.'

You could call it magic.

Yates relaxes on location with producer David Heyman.

NEWT SCAMANDER

turns secret agent

Newt Scamander has become talk of the town. He has released his instructive guide *Fantastic Beasts and Where to Find Them* — through wizarding publishers Obscurus Books — to great success and his reputation has soared. While this has instilled more confidence in the reclusive wizard, he isn't a happy man, for publication has brought some undesired side effects.

'In between the end of movie one and the beginning of movie two, Newt has found himself, very reluctantly, famous,' explains J.K. Rowling. 'And, he really hates it. This is a man who's happiest alone in a jungle, dealing with some fearsome creature that no other wizard would want to go near, and now people want his autograph, and that's hideous for him. He thought his book was going to protect and save creatures and educate his fellow wizards.'

If anything, his personal life is even more of a mess. He hasn't heard from Tina in months. What he needs, even if he isn't quite aware of this yet, is a new adventure.

Thankfully, to make sense of Newt's tribulations, Rowling's enjoyably eccentric creation remains in the capable hands of star Eddie Redmayne. And the actor is delighted to have the opportunity to 'push the edges' of this unconventional hero.

Despite the first film's success, there was to be no resting on magical laurels. If anything, as he began the sequel, he was even more aware of the responsibility he carried. Rowling was now writing Newt Scamander with the thirty-six-year-old fully in mind.

'What I love about Newt is that he's not easy,' says the British actor. 'With the first film, David Yates said to me that he wanted to explore his "knottiness". And Jo has extended that into the second film. He's still true to himself: he's not trying to please anybody. Being "knotty" means making sure you investigate the harder edges as well as the soft ones.'

Redmayne came to the first film fresh off winning an Oscar playing Stephen Hawking in *The Theory of Everything*. He returns for the second having given voice to a plucky if dim-witted caveman named Dug in the stop-motion comedy *Early Man*. No one could ever accuse the London-born, Eton- and Cambridge-educated actor of a lack of versatility.

Yet with all the promotional activity over the last two years, he has never really stopped being Newt. 'He sort of sits, burning inside you a little bit,' he says. 'An ember of Newt is sitting there.' As it will for three more films.

After being a very odd fish out of water, the sequel will show us Newt in his natural habitat. He has created a life for himself in London, and is still true to his passion for beasts. He remains a lone wolf.

'Newt is genuinely happy in his own, to other people, slightly odd world,' says Rowling. 'He's

Top: Newt and Tina on the streets of Paris *Above*: Eddie practices his wand technique between takes. *Above right*: Newt's Ministry of Magic permit; *(inset)* another wanted poster for Newt, this time in French!

having a fulfilled existence, he's making his own moral choices in an arena where he's very comfortable. However, during this movie he's forced to accept that there's no hiding from the larger struggle going on among wizard kind. It touches too many people he cares about.'

With the rise of Grindelwald, says Redmayne, the world is now a far more conflicted place. 'Newt's been pulled in different directions. He is realizing that although he's always taken his own route through life, there come moments when you have to choose a path.'

One such path will be offered by his older brother Theseus, a markedly different character to Newt. More conventionally successful,

and naturally charming, a war hero who has risen to the upper echelons of the Ministry of Magic. Theseus is now on the frontline of the fight against Grindelwald, and the Ministry will demand Newt help them track down Credence — and his Obscurus — before the Dark wizard can get to him.

'Newt is his own man and Theseus is the establishment,' says Turner, summarizing the brothers' complicated and often frosty relations.

When we first find Newt amid the bureaucratic splendour of the Ministry in London, he is in the company of the beautiful Leta Lestrange. Leta may be about to marry Theseus, but she and Newt share their own history.

One of Redmayne's favourite sequences in the new film is a flashback to Newt's schooldays at Hogwarts, where we get a glimpse of how he first came to meet Leta. 'You realize that these two, Leta and Newt, are connected through being outsiders. Frankly, they're both damaged in some way.'

Hogwarts is also where Newt discovered his calling for Magizoology. We spy him in a tiny cupboard-turned-menagerie where he is trying to heal a damaged raven chick — ravens are the Lestrange family emblem. 'It's almost like he's a magnet for damaged people or damaged beasts,' says Redmayne. 'What he is best at is helping.'

Most significantly, the famous School of Witchcraft and Wizardry is where Newt first encountered the legendary Albus Dumbledore. The bond between Newt and his former teacher of Defence Against the Dark Arts is another complicated relationship for the new film to explore. Played by Jude Law, this is a much younger, more dapper Dumbledore than the venerable headmaster from the Harry Potter films. In contrast to Harry's grandfatherly bond with Dumbledore, there isn't such a great age difference with Newt.

'What I loved about Dumbledore was that twinkle in his eye,' says Redmayne. 'He has an extraordinary wisdom, but also a wry humour to him. I was so excited when Jude was cast, because he's such a playful actor. You really get to mess around with him.'

From Redmayne's perspective, Dumbledore can see much of himself in Newt's impetuous spirit, and his awkwardness. 'Newt isn't everyone's cup of tea, and I'm sure Dumbledore wasn't exactly many of the staff at Hogwarts' cup of tea.' They are both people who refuse to jump to orders.

Since Newt left Hogwarts (under complicated circumstances) they have remained in touch, but he is well aware Dumbledore is also manipulating him when he presents Newt with yet another path. Strolling home to his London apartment, Newt is Apparated on to the roof of St Paul's Cathedral for a clandestine rendezvous, as Dumbledore persuades Newt to secretly head to Paris to save Credence.

'Newt is too wily to be exploited,' says Redmayne. 'It is a level playing field, so Dumbledore can only achieve what he needs by appealing to their friendship.'

'Newt is one of the few to call Dumbledore on what he does to other people,' adds Rowling. 'That's what's so interesting to me about their relationship, because I want someone to call Dumbledore on his secretiveness, and his manipulation, and I want to hear his answers.'

With a hint of espionage entering the wizarding world, Newt takes on the guise of a magical secret agent, but instead of gadgets he utilizes a case filled with beasts. This covert mission to Paris will also offer him a chance to revive his friendship with Jacob, who has unexpectedly appeared in London with Queenie.

Tossing one final stone in the stilled pond of Newt's life, he learns that Tina also happens to be in Paris, in search of Credence, but wants nothing to do with Newt.

Between films, Newt's romantic life has taken a nosedive.

'Newt has very little social capacity, let alone with people he finds attractive. He managed to articulate himself enough when standing on those docks in New York, to make it clear to Tina that he had feelings for her, and she clearly did too. There was a world where he thought it might be happily ever after,' notes Redmayne.

Whichever world that was, it wasn't the Wizarding World, where happily ever after is the stuff of cliché. To begin with, Newt has been banned from travelling.

'His travel documents have been taken away by the Ministry under slightly suspicious circumstances,' explains Redmayne. 'All Newt wants is to go back to New York, find Tina, give her a copy of the book, and to see her again, frankly.'

Below: Newt emerges into Nicolas Flamel's house.

Newt is accompanied along the familiar green marble-tiled corridor of the Ministry of Magic by a new character: Leta Lestrange (Zoë Kravitz). *Inset:* Ready for action.

If there is one thing Newt can rely on in life, even if they are highly unpredictable, it is the fantastic beasts. And his mission to Paris will involve plenty of new species as well as familiar friends.

'The Niffler's back,' says Redmayne, 'and has had babies. There's not only one scene-stealer; there's now an entire family of them. And there are new creatures, including the Kelpie, who's an underwater horse. You get to see Newt sub-aqua! You know, I'm curious to see how that goes.'

COLLEEN ATWOOD ON NEWT

'Our hero has a new look: more urbanized, more grown up and comfortable with who he is.' Redmayne and Atwood had even discussed dropping the bow tie, but it was too much a part of who he is.

In the first film, Atwood figured Newt had been living in the wilderness, and his costume represented his attempts to blend in back among civilization. 'The trick then was to make Newt's clothes a little mismatched, ill-fitting, to give a feeling of quirkiness. His dirty peacock blue coat defined him.'

Now, he's become a publishing success, and his looks is a little slicker. 'The materials of his suit are much more refined,' says Atwood. 'It fits better. He is still set apart, but also more of the time and place.'

As Newt is working undercover his overcoat is a subtle shade of heathery grey rather than peacock blue. And taking her inspiration from magician's jackets, Atwood lined his new coat with secret pockets, where he might stow a Bowtruckle, or handy vials of curative elixir.

They had at least been communicating via letter, but Tina has stopped replying. Newt worries this might be down to certain comments he made about Aurors. Tina, after all, is an Auror. The truth is that her silence is due to a classic misunderstanding. She has seen a copy of magical magazine *Spellbound* picturing Newt's book launch, in which he appeared alongside Leta, Theseus and a beaming Bunty. But the caption mistakenly claims it is Newt who is getting married to Leta, rather than his brother.

'So unfortunately,' says Redmayne, 'we start in a place of complete miscommunication between two people who already can't communicate.'

As an actor, he loves that so much of this huge adventure is the story of two people who keep missing each other with 'words and language and emotion', yet somehow still find one another.

'Even though they start the film at loggerheads, they naturally have each other's back. That is what is brilliant about Jo. Yes, these characters are imaginative, yes they have magic, but they are grounded.'

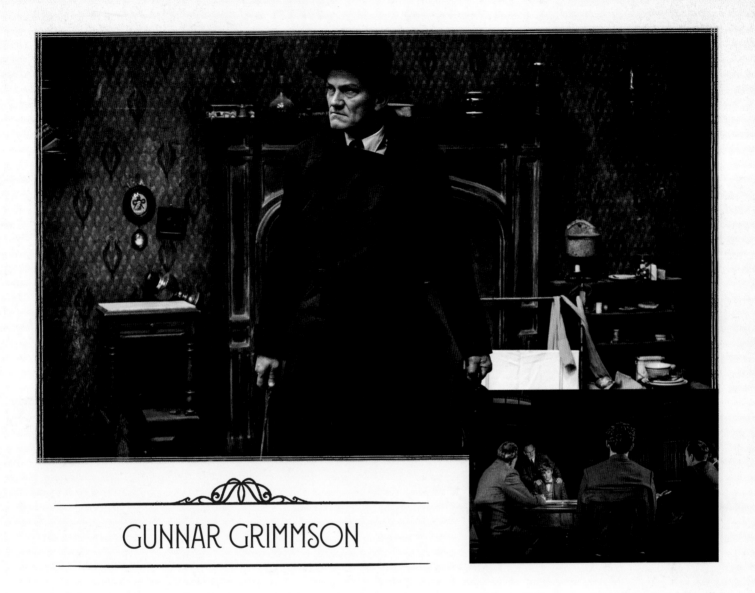

GUNNAR GRIMMSON

As scarred and brutal as his name suggests, Gunnar Grimmson is the polar opposite of everything the Magizoologist hero stands for. He hunts down beasts rather than rescues them, taking a cruel pleasure in his task. In short, he is the anti-Newt — his nemesis. And now he's tracking Newt's movements through the avenues of Paris.

'He's hired by London's Ministry of Magic to hunt down Credence,' says actor Ingvar Eggert Sigurðsson, who naturally feels his character is misunderstood. 'To me he's a good guy, but not possibly to the audience, and definitely not to Newt. He hates him. They have some kind of past. Grimmson is very skilled at hunting down *dangerous* beasts.'

The fifty-four-year-old Icelandic star —who had previously appeared is such English-language films as *Everest* and *Justice League* — would also like to point out that his Harry Potter-obsessed kids were delighted their father had been cast in this world. Even if he does happen to be playing one of J.K. Rowling's more despicable inventions.

By Grimmson's twisted logic, magical beasts represent a great risk to the world, none more so than an Obscurus. 'So he's the right man for the job,' states Sigurðsson.

Sensible enough not to stalk Paris dressed like a big game hunter, he blends in with the crowd, much more like a spy or mercenary, with a long overcoat and boots giving him what costume designer Colleen Atwood calls, 'a really sinister noir edge.'

He also uses magic to literally blend in. It pays to keep an eye on nearby walls — they may have ears and eyes, and unpleasant intentions.

Top: The fearsome beast hunter Gunnar Grimmson (Ingvar Eggert Sigurðsson). *Above:* Confronting Newt in the Ministry's Hearing Room with (*left to right*) ICW's Head of Incarceration, Rudolph Spielman (Wolf Roth), Newt's brother, Theseus Scamander (Callum Turner), Head of the British Auror Office, Head of Magical Law Enforcement Torquil Travers (Derek Riddell), & American Emissary to the ICW, Arnold Guzman (Cornell John).

THESEUS SCAMANDER
takes charge

You may remember mention of Newt's older brother Theseus amid the hurly-burly of the first *Fantastic Beasts*. Theseus and Newt are quite different. The older Scamander is a bit of a golden boy. A First World War hero, he has since become Head of the British Auror Office at the Ministry of Magic in London. As self-assured as Newt is socially awkward, he has also recently become betrothed to Leta Lestrange — his brother's former classmate.

'He has decided to fight the good fight, and climbed high up at the Ministry,' explains Callum Turner, the London-born young actor charged with giving us a different perspective on the Scamander family. 'That is the difference between the two brothers — Theseus is part of the establishment.'

Like most people his age, the twenty-eight-year-old Turner grew up with Harry Potter. He was ten when his mum bought him the first book, and he admits he wasn't much of a reader. 'But I just blasted through it,' he recalls, 'and then went to bed most nights hoping that one of Hedwig's friends would drop a letter in saying I'm due at Hogwarts. Now, that has kind of come true.'

When he auditioned, the brief script pages he was given referred to the character only as Theo. It didn't take too much detective work to figure out who he is. Turner just typed 'Theo' into the *Pottermore* site and 'Theseus' immediately came up.

Eight years Newt's senior (although Turner is nine years *younger* than Eddie Redmayne), Theseus is less eccentric to the eye. 'Generally, he is part of the world, dressed in a fine suit,' says Turner. 'But there are tiny similarities between his and Newt's look: ankle swingers, a pocket square, these wizard-ish touches in the shapes of the lapel and the collar.'

Although he had small parts in horror revamp *Victor Frankenstein* and video game adaptation *Assassin's Creed*, until now Turner's film career has focused on intimate, indie films such as *Queen and Country* and *The Only Living Boy in New York*. He had never experienced anything on this scale before. Luckily, he and Eddie Redmayne had an instant rapport. As fate would have it, they had both grown up in Chelsea, literally ten minutes apart. Both learned to swim at the same pool.

'It was in the stars,' says Turner. 'If you're from a certain part of the world there's a similar energy. We bonded very quickly.'

As a wizard, you also get to go to wand school. 'You get a bumper course,' he says. 'You use a wand like a whip, that was the main thing that stuck with me. You're sending energy down the arm. But you're also supposed to be very good at it, so it shouldn't take too much effort. At the beginning my movements were a bit too much.'

As for his wand, well, according to Turner it's simply better than Eddie's. Turner has a handsome wand with a tortoise shell handle. 'I think Eddie was a bit jealous,' he adds.

His relationship with said wand, however, has not been without its mishaps. 'I actually broke it on the first outing. For which, actually, I blame Eddie. He just flipped his out and put me off, and then mine smashed on the ground.'

While tolerating his predilection for magical beasts, Newt has long been a worry to his brother. Still, Theseus and Leta did attend the launch of his new book. And with Theseus having been chosen to help hunt down Grindelwald, Newt's talents might actually be of use. With the Dark wizard fixed on tracking down the Obscurial hiding out in Paris, Torquil Travers, the Head of Magical Law Enforcement, presses the younger Scamander to help them intercept Credence.

Even when Newt refuses, Theseus asks him to be his best man.

On the surface, Theseus and Leta's romance looks a fine match. As far as Theseus is concerned they have fallen in love, they're engaged, and things are going well in their life.

Yet unbeknownst to the older Scamander, Leta has her own store of secrets that threaten to derail the forthcoming wedding.

Above: Theseus stands with a team of British and French Aurors, preparing to confront Grindelwald; *(inset)* Theseus Scamander, Head of the British Auror Office. *Opposite (top to bottom):* the Scamander brothers in action; David Yates directs Turner and Kravitz on the set of the grandly named Ministère des Affaires Magiques de la France; Theseus and Newt stand together in the amphitheatre.

Newt's older brother has a more by-the-book feel of someone trying to do everything the right way. 'So the shape of his clothes is quite similar to his brother,' says Atwood, 'but the way they fit has a more classic sense of the period, while Newt's is a bit off-centre.'

MIRAPHORA MINA & EDUARDO LIMA — GRAPHIC DESIGN

British graphic artist Miraphora Mina goes all the way back to *Harry Potter and the Philosopher's Stone*. Her Brazilian partner Eduardo Lima came onboard for *Harry Potter and the Chamber of Secrets*. Together they have defined the typographical style of the wizarding world, officially founding MinaLima Design in 2010 (which gets an honourary fictional mention on a poster in *Harry Potter and The Deathly Hallows - Part 1*.)

Graphic design essentially covers any prop or decoration that involves printed words or design. For instance, the Marauder's Map, or the *Daily Prophet*, or every single box and label for the sweets at Honeydukes.

'Everything snowballs if you have a shop in the film,' says Lima: 'it will be full of products, which need labels and price tags, branding, point of sale, advertisements on the side of buildings. Everything is created bespoke for the movies.'

'Our scope of work ranges from making tiny individual hero props that are part of the story,' says Mina, 'to things that fill the scenic environment.'

'The films are becoming bigger and bigger,' says Lima.

Each and every item they create has its own backstory — its own logical place in this world. It needs to fit like the piece of a puzzle. 'You know when you see the wrong typeface,' says Mina, 'because it feels strange.'

The Ministry of Magic stationery, for instance, had to differ from what they devised for the same location in Harry Potter in order to reflect an earlier time period, but still be reminiscent of what it is to come.

From street signs to apothecary labels to magical stationery, they both admit Paris of 1927 has been a gift. There are opportunities to design 'kind of excessively,' says Mina. The styles of the time, Art Nouveau with its curvilinear flourishes and its next-of-kin Art Deco, begged to be put to use in the wizarding world. With Art Nouveau having been adopted as the look of the

Ministère des Affaires Magiques de la France, they let that inform how they designed the paperwork and ephemera of the French Ministry of Magic. 'We have carried that through, it's playful and kind of poetic in its visuals,' says Mina.

On any project, the first thing they do is to cover their office with reference material, immersing themselves in the era. 'What was interesting about both New York and now Paris is that you see the old styles as well,' says Lima. 'It was all a bit messy. The transition between eras is never clean.'

They went on a recce to Paris in search of details that no one else would be interested in: advertising, illustrations, wallpaper designs, and printing techniques. How things were authentically manufactured in 1927 was vitally important, as they would attempt to replicate it in the same way.

The dedication to detail is astonishing. Nothing is left to chance. Every typographic element of every set has been thought through and prepared in case David Yates's camera happens to pass by.

Just as on the last film, they had to bear in mind that American English isn't English English, and French is most *definitely* not English. What's more, their French had to be the French vernacular of 1927. Hence they hired a French graphic co-ordinator to monitor any typography *en Francais*.

'That's challenging, doing things in other languages,' says Lima. 'And there was a tiny bit of Chinese in this too.'

The point is that everything must be anchored in reality before it is shifted into the wizarding world, where magical flourishes must be subtle

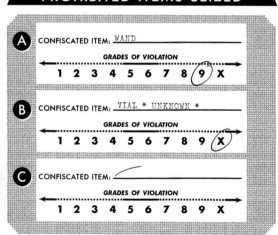

and clever — and often painstaking to achieve.

Like the *Daily Prophet* and *The New York Ghost* before it, French wizarding daily *Le Cri de la Gargouille* has been entirely stocked with stories invented by Mina and Lima and their team.

'We're given the headline,' says Mina, 'then we'll build a world around that. Always trying to give readers the opportunity to place where we are and what's happened. Sometimes we'll look at what's happening in the real world at the time, other things going on in France and Europe that might be relevant.'

It is another way to draw parallels between the drama and J.K. Rowling's real-world themes like the rise of fascism that was happening in Europe. With no books to refer to for the *Fantastic Beasts* films, the author is an indispensable resource, even filling them in on details that might influence future films.

As well as the wealth of incidental elements, there are those very specific story or 'hero' props to design. For instance, ancient wizarding tomes like *The Predictions of Tycho Dodonus* and Nicolas Flamel's magical book, and Credence's all-important certificate of adoption, which has guided

him, and in effect, the entire film to Paris.

'With the adoption paper, we had done maybe three or four and sent them in,' laughs Lima. 'A message came back saying, "Oh, we need thirty new ones." Because there was a scene where Credence gets all angry and crumples it up.'

'When you've specially aged them, that's really what takes the time,' says Mina.

'Because you sand down the paper until you have little holes in it like wormholes,' says Lima.

Only then is it perfect.

A PUBLISHING SENSATION

Given we would see a finished copy of Newt Scamander's *Fantastic Beasts and Where to Find Them* in the new film, the graphic design team of Miraphora Mina and Eduardo Lima had the peculiar task of designing the book within the films of the book.

'It's different from the prop you see in the first Harry Potter film,' observes Lima, in reference to Harry's copy, 'this is the original, the first edition.'

'In 1927, it has just been published,' says Mina. 'And obviously, we had to give it a little cheeky twist to the wizarding world. It would have been a little bit more conservative if it had been published by a Muggle publisher in twenties London.'

They have stuck to the same colour scheme of black and gold as we see in the first Harry Potter film, the idea being it is one of those classics that gets on the curriculum every year. However, this plush first edition has an entirely different cover design.

'It's quite busy,' says Lima, 'with a series of decorative, geometric patterns, on the brink of Art Deco. If you look closely, though, every single piece of that pattern is a beast.'

With every prop, the designers have to consider: what is the backstory behind it? Even when they were doing the potion books in Harry Potter they established a series of different editions that had been published through the years.

Published by Obscurus Books of Diagon Alley, the launch of Newt's book has caused such a stir it has even made the wizarding magazine *Spellbound*. A moving picture from the event held at Flourish and Blotts bookshop, also of Diagon Alley, is inside its pages.

Flourish and Blotts will be familiar to readers of Harry Potter. 'It is actually referred to in the books so we made the assumption that it would be launched there,' says Mina.

'Early on, we go through the script and work out what all the moving pictures will be,' she continues. Anything more elaborate than a portrait will require them to do a mock-up of what needs to be shot. 'We then give that back to the assistant directors and say something like, '"We're going to need a moving picture of Tina doing this, and something for a wanted poster or, rather, more like *thirty* things for wanted posters."'

For the moving picture of Newt and friends at his launch party, a picture that will have unfortunate repercussions when Tina sees it, they actually built a set for Flourish and Blotts. Even on the scale of a moving picture, the level of detail is incredible. As far as Mina and Lima are concerned there is no such thing as background detail. 'Our ethos,' says Mina, 'is to apply the same amount of precision to every level of the film to create the authenticity.'

If you are in a bookshop, they realized, you need to think about the other books. For the different sections of Flourish and Blotts, they went back through all the magical subjects that have been mentioned in the wizarding world. 'All the signs on the end of the bookcases relate to the different departments,' says Lima. There is even a shelf devoted to Occlumency and Arithmancy.

Funnily enough, the one section they didn't include was fiction.

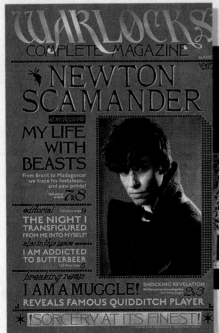

Opposite: Newt is supported at his book launch by his brother, Theseus, and his brother's fiancée, Leta, together with his assistant, Bunty (Victoria Yeates). *Above:* Graphic props advertising the book launch and the book itself plus *(far left)* Warlock magazine, which promises an interview with the now-famous wizard. *Left:* An author's view of the signing.

QUEENIE GOLDSTEIN

Queenie is not herself at all. Her entire outlook on life was transformed when Newt Scamander crashed into the relatively subdued magical existence she shared with her sister Tina in a New York brownstone, with a case full of beasts and a humble Brooklyn baker in tow. A world of excitement and possibility had opened up. Not least the possibility of love for the beautiful, young witch gifted — and cursed — with Legilimency: the power to decipher thoughts.

'In the first film, she had this real innocence and vulnerability and joy and excitement,' says Alison Sudol, 'there was this adventure suddenly happening in her life. Then meeting Jacob was just wonderful. It was really delicious exploring all that.'

Between films, Queenie has got herself into something of a fix. Wary of discovery by the outside world, MACUSA have stringent laws about any kind of interaction with No-Majs. The notion of marrying one is outrageous. But Queenie has taken it upon herself to reverse the effects of Jacob's Obliviation in the hope of doing just that — marrying him.

'By the time of the second movie they have been in a relationship for a while,' she explains. 'There is a bit of desperation, and it pushes her to make, perhaps, not the wisest of choices.'

Her actions have a caused a rift between the two sisters. Furthermore, with Jacob unwilling to break wizarding regulations, Queenie has placed him under a spell and whisked him to Europe where marriage to a No-Maj is permitted.

After Newt restores the befuddled baker to his normal faculties, there is a blazing row, and a deeply ashamed Queenie storms off to find Tina in Paris, where she will fall under Grindelwald's poisonous influence.

Importantly, we still need to believe that in her core she is the same person. 'You need to stay with her,' Sudol says, 'even if it hurts.' This includes some pretty tough scenes with Dan Fogler as her now ex-fiancé, Jacob.

'Thankfully, Dan and I are really good friends now,' says Sudol. 'We live three blocks away from each other in Brooklyn, and I love his family. It would be harder to do that with someone that I trusted less. He takes it very well, right on the chin.'

There is also the burden that comes with her 'gift' of Legilimency — the double-edged ability to intuit (rather than directly read) the thoughts of others. Sudol remarks, 'What I didn't know, which is funny because Queenie didn't either, is how powerful a trait it is in the wizarding world. Then I saw this one fan video and was like, "*Oh.*" But it had to seem natural. She wouldn't need to think about it.'

What has been a thrill in returning — apart from catching up with old friends, of course — is that much of the dramatic action spins through the streets of a Paris at the tail end of the tumultuous twenties. 'What Stuart [Craig] has done

with the sets,' says Sudol, a fan at heart, 'it's everything you want and expect in the wizarding world's version of Paris. I mean, it's so detailed, so beautiful, so authentic.'

In Paris, vulnerable and alone, Queenie is scooped up by Grindelwald's shadowy gang of acolytes, and Sudol has been so impressed by how J.K. Rowling depicts the Dark wizard not as an ogre or outright villain but as a master manipulator. Grindelwald knows the way to get to Queenie is through her big heart, and he begins telling her everything she wants to hear.

'He's also a bit flirty,' says Sudol. 'It's the age-old thing of the good girl getting swayed by the bad boy.'

On first reading the script, Sudol admits that the complex journey that Queenie takes came as a shock. Having given it some thought, she now sees that there was no other way for the character to go. 'It's a lovely idea that she and Jacob fall madly in love and they have lots of children. But where is the drama in that? This is an exploration of the uninitiated maiden's descent in to the underworld...'

Top: Queenie is under the weather in Paris. *Above:* Queenie is given plenty to think about by Grindelwald. *Inset:* Queenie's travelling case. *Opposite, top to bottom:* Queenie and Jacob surprise Newt with an unexpected visit; Queenie arrives in Paris; *(inset)* Queenie wears Atwood's plaid dress costume with lovely butterfly detail.

COLLEEN ATWOOD ON QUEENIE

'We felt that Queenie had grown up in this film. For some reason, in the first fitting Alison said, "I just thought I'd be in plaid" and that worked.'

'I felt Queenie would come to London and go, "Well, what do they wear in England? I think they wear tartan,"' explains Sudol. 'She brings her own elegant, Art Deco twist to plaid. I also thought she would be wearing more jewellery, be more sophisticated.'

Atwood provided a moth pendant, and they played around with the shape and colour until it resembled a butterfly. The idea was to hint toward Queenie's transformation. 'She's in a butterfly sort of transformation,' says Sudol, 'but it's also the moth — the butterfly of the night.'

JACOB KOWALSKI
has relationship problems

When we last saw Dan Fogler's loveable Jacob Kowalski, he had stepped into a magical downpour to wash away all the wonderful memories of his encounter with witches and wizards. As a No-Maj, he had recognized it was necessary to wash his memory clean of all the extraordinary things he had encountered in the company of Magizoologist Newt Scamander, not to mention the heart-stopping witch Queenie Goldstein. But wait, at the *very* end of the first film, hadn't Queenie slipped into Jacob's bustling new bakery, where his pastries bore an uncanny resemblance to Erumpents, Demiguises and Nifflers?

In any case, Newt does not expect to have Queenie and Jacob as houseguests in his London bachelor pad at the beginning of the sequel. Furthermore, it doesn't take long for the English wizard to detect that relations between the lovebirds are not as magical as they appear to be. Actually, that they are rather *too magical*. 'Jacob is being unnaturally jolly,' says Fogler, 'I'm a little bit *too* happy. It turns out Queenie has put me under her spell.'

By which he means she has *really* put him under a spell.

Never having been in a franchise before, Fogler has found the opportunity to continue a character arc really satisfying. 'Jacob is like an authentic family member,' he adds. He thinks of the new film not as a sequel so much as the next part in one continuous story.

'What J.K. Rowling does, which is so amazing, is that like in the Harry Potter movies, these characters get older, their look changes, their whole vibe changes. Here the characters are getting a little bit older, a little bit more complex.'

Those early, spellbound scenes, in particular, were great fun to play. He got to devise an entire slapstick comedy routine, only with this complicated subtext. Under the effects of the spell, Jacob is really not himself. He is almost drunk on magic, idiotically pouring salt all over the dinner table and poking himself in the eye, with a nobody's-home expression plastered on his face. An appalled Newt swiftly remedies the situation. Jacob is understandably upset with his fiancée and a very non-magical row ensues, resulting in an embarrassed, heartbroken Queenie running off into the London night. 'It's great,' says Fogler, 'it has its roots in real relationship dynamics.'

Fogler had no trouble getting back into the mindset of this humble baker with hidden depths. It was simply a case of putting on the costume (a newly upgraded suit and overcoat combo care of his newfound affluence) and reapplying the pencil

moustache. 'I just look at myself in the mirror: "Yep, there it is..."' All he needs to do is give an extra twang to his native Brooklyn accent and he's back in business.

Jacob joins Newt on his mission to the French capital, desperate to make things right with Queenie. But compounding Jacob's relationship problems, he will have a serious rival for Queenie's attentions in the shape of Grindelwald. For, having fled to Paris, Queenie will fall into the charismatic wizard's orbit.

'Things are getting serious on many levels,' says Fogler. 'But the beautiful thing about Jacob is that, even though he finds himself in the middle of chaos, he tries to do the right thing. He's going to help Newt until the end of his journey. His heart is so big that he can't help but help people.'

If there is an upside to his predicament, it is the chance to renew his friendship with Newt. 'Their relationship is iconic,' observes Fogler. 'It's like Han and Luke, Sherlock and Watson, and Laurel and Hardy. There are moments there,

Top to bottom: The Portkey comes in handy after Jacob suffers from magically induced travel sickness; it's all smiles for Dan, with Eddie and his director. *Opposite, top to bottom:* Newt and Jacob set off in search of a Portkey; Jacob gets serious when Newt, Tina and he decide what to do about Kama.

where you look at us, it could almost be in black and white. We're two different sides of the spectrum, both physically and personality wise. Newt is book smart and I am street smart.'

Correspondingly, it has been a joy to rekindle his double-act with co-star Eddie Redmayne. 'We're both fans of that era of comedy and we get to put it in action. We know the characters so well that we didn't really rehearse. We just flowed.'

Once again, Jacob's reacquaintance with Newt and his collection of capricious beasts, as well as the fresh dangers lurking beneath the streets of Paris, will have a transformative effect on the baker.

'As much as he tries to get out, they keep pulling him back in. He's the Al Pacino of the wizarding world!' says Fogler.

And for all his effort and bravery, he still doesn't get a wand. 'I really want one,' adds Fogler. 'Maybe I'll get one down the line. But, you know, I'm magic on the inside. I've got a soul of gold.'

COLLEEN ATWOOD ON JACOB

'In his own mind he [Jacob] has become a successful guy,' says Atwood. 'So his suit finally fits and all of the pieces are the same fabric, where before they were three, totally separate things. I always try to give the actor a little something to entertain himself with and we made the top of his shoes out of the same material as his suit, to tie it all together. When they're in the same costume the whole movie it can be hard, so you try to keep it fun for them.'

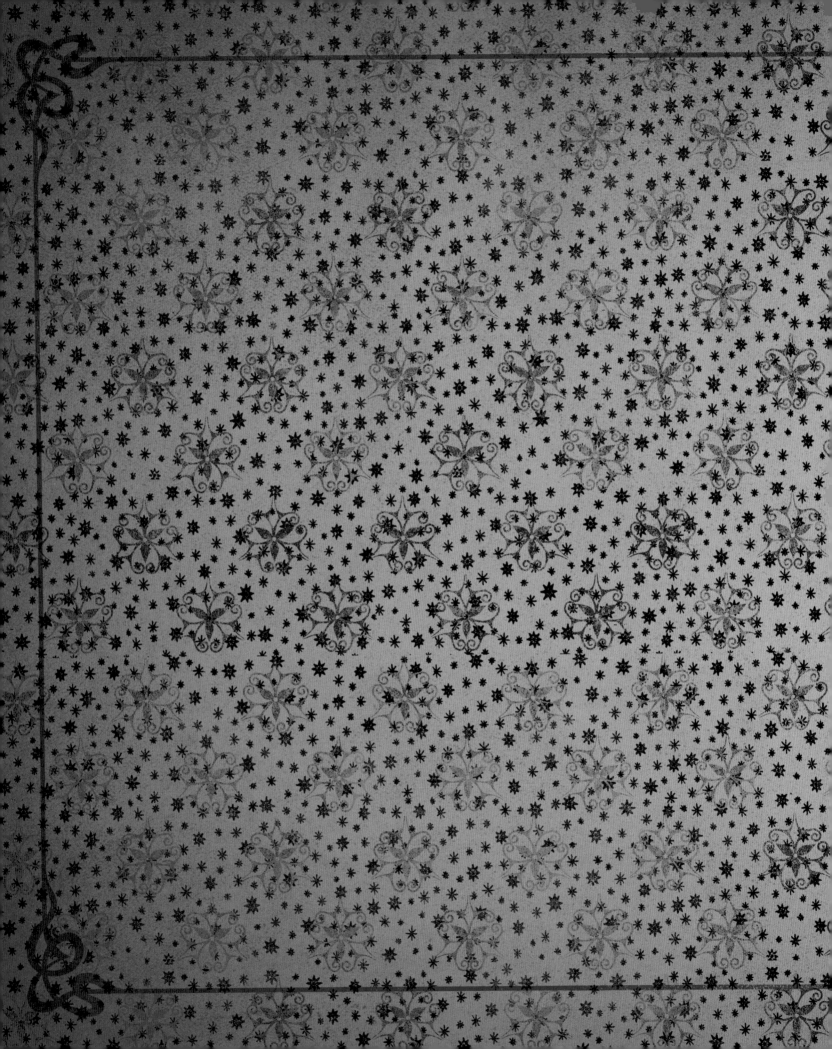

A CELLAR FULL of BEASTS

NEWT'S BASEMENT

One of the new film's most extraordinary visions, Newt's basement is a fantastical extension of the portable beast preserve he carried around in his case.

'While he uses his suitcase out on adventures, we now get to see his home,' says Eddie Redmayne. 'Walking onto that set was pretty breathtaking.'

Newt being Newt, when you go down into the basement, says Redmayne, you enter into an 'absolutely mindboggling' menagerie. Here is where you will find Newt's true personality expressed. Downstairs, below decks, is the nerve-centre of his universe of beast management. This is also where he lives.

'He's a man much more at home travelling through the jungle,' says Redmayne. 'I felt that he would still go and live in his hammock down in the basement.'

'Jo describes it as an animal hospital,' explains production designer Stuart Craig. 'And in the set dressing we've tried very much to illustrate that. That is tending creatures as opposed to being a rescue home, which is what his suitcase was, really. It's a subtle distinction.'

According to Craig's structural conceit, the detail is still of a basement beneath a London house with brick arches and pillars, but what is magical is the extent of it. It seems to go to infinity almost in every direction. While through the arches can be seen different environments to suit the creature within.

Concept art by Dermot Power reveals the multi-coloured views of magically maintained beast environments.

Above: Newt's living area in his basement – note the miniature Bowtruckle tree on his desk. *Inset:* Newt's assistant, Bunty (Victoria Yeates). *Opposite, top to bottom:* Newt's crowded desk includes old Hogwarts school books, application permits to travel (stamped "denied" by the Ministry of Magic), and page proofs for his book from his publisher, Obscurus Books; part of Stuart Craig's fantastic set design for Newt's basement; a sign warns 'Not to use on humans'.

'We come back to the idea of taking something real and detailing it in a real way so it has complete credibility,' says Craig. 'Then what is incredible is the scale of it, the vastness of it, the exaggeration. Like Escher, who is often used as an inspiration for movie sets.'

M.C. Escher was the early twentieth-century Dutch artist famed for his explorations of perspective and geometry in woodcut illustrations of endless stairways.

'Stuart always steps sideways from the script and does something you would never think of,' says concept artist Dermot Power, who works in close proximity with the revered production designer, and lent his own perspective to the basement. 'If somebody said it was a veterinary hospital you would think that everything is lateral and flat. You would walk from this room to that room. But Stuart flipped it around and made it a tall, narrow basement with different levels. It is the exact opposite of what the script seemed to suggest.'

Even without its digital extensions, the actual set was awesome to behold, soaring three stories into the air, a dizzying geometric, three-dimensional maze made of arches, walls and stairways

rising out of shot. Through these crisscrossing, stone stairways, which connect with the flat above, Newt's interior design is a little reminiscent of his days at Hogwarts. 'It is Victorian classical in style rather than Gothic,' explains Craig, 'but nonetheless the spirit of it is the school.'

More bizarrely still, at the centre of the basement floor can be found the same shed we saw within the case in the first film. It is another of Craig's instinctive leftfield tilts to J.K. Rowling's concepts without the need to offer any concrete or even magical explanation — not that there hasn't been plenty of debate in other departments over the inter-dimensionality of a garden shed.

'The shed being there is classic Stuart,' remarks Power. 'It's like the monolith in *2001*, this weird shed in the middle of this space.'

'It is quite an intriguing concept,' says Craig; the shed had been in and out of designs. 'Anyway, seeing is believing. If we get the detail right, which I am sure we have, then it will have its own credibility.'

Newt tends to his injured and vulnerable beasts with the help of his assistant Bunty (played by Victoria Yeates, of *Call the Midwife* fame), who has a painfully obvious crush on her boss, to which he naturally remains completely oblivious.

The Magizoologist is truly in his element interacting with various beasts, including an entire family of Nifflers, for which Pierre Bohanna's prop making department made a glass feeding bottle for the babies (about the cutest thing ever). 'It had about six teats on it,' he says.

There were also a set of Niffler feeding boxes, and a very small Bowtruckle tree for Newt's desk. 'I don't want to use the term Bonsai tree,'

says Bohanna, 'because it was supposed to be a cutting off a Bowtruckle tree to give Pickett somewhere to go and rest. But, to be honest, it looks like a Bonsai tree.'

As well as two generations of Nifflers and the Bowtruckles, Newt is currently caring for a family of Mooncalves, a distressed Kelpie, and an Augurey — a mournful looking bird, like a cross between and owl and a vulture.

WARNING
DO NOT USE ON HUMANS

'We did a lot of research into contemporary zoologists and vets,' says set decorator Anna Pinnock, also keen to fuse the real and magical for maximum effect. That also means the two sides of Newt — the strict dedication and his off-centeredness. 'David Yates wanted to make Newt seem a lot more focused and recognizably professional, immersed in the care of his creatures, practical in his skills while also keeping his eccentricity and special magical abilities with the creatures as evident as possible.'

For the specific fabric of the set, Pinnock found some re-purposed equipment to express the uniqueness of Newt's veterinary practice.

'We created an X-ray machine based on what was happening in the era,' says Bohanna. Magic and science are blended together, with Bohanna even providing some radiation suits hanging from coat-hooks.

In amongst the jumble of tables and desks, and pseudo-scientific equipment, the graphic design department contributed labels for potion bottles, sketches and a pile of notebooks that Newt has been collating. 'He has maps and charts,' says graphic designer Eduardo Lima. 'And we brought back many of the things we designed for the first film. There were specific notes from the book he was writing.'

'You're always trying to think about the personality behind the thing that you're having to create,' explains Mina. 'We know he's very logical, but also impulsive like a mad professor.'

As Craig mentioned, through the large arches — given just a hint of the Moorish curves of the Alhambra palace in Spain — placed up and down the full height and breadth of the basement, we will catch glimpses of creature habitats.

'Each of these alcoves replaces what in the suitcase was all those biomes,' explains Power. 'But the difference this time is that they won't walk into them. You are observing them.'

Within the fixed architecture of the basement the environments were to be less painterly and more realistic. Those alcoves we catch only in passing would naturally fall into the remit of the visual effects department, already responsible for the beasts. But for two alcoves that could be clearly seen in the background of the shots Power conceptualized something more detailed.

'There is one shot where the Augurey starts up from an arch behind the shed, and the

camera spins around as he flies about and interacts with Newt,' he says. 'Because he is an Irish bird that is a portent of bad things, I used my local church in Ireland.'

With the help of Google Maps, Power depicted the exact graveyard and church where he grew up. 'It's like an in-joke,' he says. 'You'll see some miserable Irish conditions in there.'

Framed behind Jacob can be seen a habitat belonging to a family of Mooncalves, with their big eyes and spindly legs. In the first film, the Mooncalves lived within the case on a floating planetoid.

With good design you feel there is a life outside of the frame.

Arguably the highlight of the entire basement sequence is the moment Newt plunges into a large pool to put a bridle on a Kelpie (an underwater creature) who needs a drop of salve in an open cut— a tricky business.

'The solution,' says Power, 'was to fill one alcove up with water in which the Kelpie floated, while behind it the water falls back infinitely into the darkness.'

What might seem peculiar is that the surface of the water is vertical rather than horizontal, filling an entire arch.

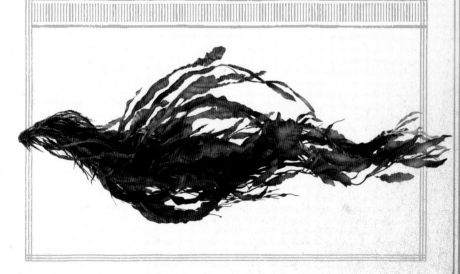

DESIGNING A NEW SET OF BEASTS

For all the twists and turns of Grindelwald's evil machinations, a host of unquestionably fantastic beasts remain the heart of the story. Each successive film will introduce us to a wonderful array of new creations, cooked up with J.K. Rowling's subtle blend of real animals and mythological beings, seasoned with a flare for the adorable that is all her own.

Indeed, for Rowling, Newt's kindred relationship has only become more important. 'I've got a hero who is interested in saving an aspect of the magical world that, at this period, virtually no one else cared about,' she says. 'Newt is treading this very lonely road where he says, "You know what? We are destroying something so beautiful if we let these creatures go. They are inconvenient, they get in the way, they break the Statute of Secrecy, many of you don't understand them and are really frightened of them, but we have to protect them, and I'm going to do it." And, that gets him into all kinds of trouble. And, it compounds what other people see as his oddness.'

When it comes to bringing these creatures to life on screen, Rowling's words are always the foundation. 'Both in the script, but also those descriptions found in the book of *Fantastic Beasts and Where to Find Them*,' says producer David Heyman. 'Concepts are then drawn up both by the art and the visual effects department: different artists pursuing different designs. We generate thousands of designs and gradually cull them down to the ones that we are most excited about.'

Heyman still considers the two most successful beasts of the first film were the bank-robbing Niffler and Pickett, the spindly Bowtruckle. They both have very clearly defined personalities and characters. They moved exactly as they looked like they should move. They felt natural.

With the advances in digital effects, creature creation falls under the jurisdiction of the visual effects team, headed up by visual effects supervisors Tim Burke and Christian Manz.

'It's a very collaborative process,' Manz says. 'David Yates is very generous in allowing us to come up with ideas. Obviously, you're looking at what Jo has written, but we contribute our own ideas on character or how an action sequence might progress, and David tells us what he likes and very nicely tells us what he doesn't like.'

Above: Newt rides the Kelpie. *Opposite:* Concept art by Sam Rowan of the Chupacabra on top of the Elder Wand.

An individual creature (or sequence) can keep evolving from preproduction, through the shoot, all the way through to postproduction. Key to this is the involvement of the actors, which has only increased with the second film. 'They watch pre-vis as we're developing it and they're giving us their character beats,' explains Burke. 'So we're getting Eddie saying what he would do and Katherine saying what she is up to, and we're developing the story with them. They're giving us ideas for what the creatures would do.'

Eddie Redmayne, says Burke, is now so familiar with his Nifflers and his Bowtruckles and he points out exactly how he sees them behaving. 'It's a real collaboration and they're very comfortable with it,' he says, reaching for the perfect word. 'It's actually a symbiotic process.'

For the new film, rather than lurking in (and hotfooting it from) Newt's case, the beasts are spread across the Magizoologist's voluminous basement, the seedy Circus Arcanus, and the French Ministry.

Manz starts totting up them up in his head. 'We've got a magical circus where we've got a Japanese Oni and a Kappa, which is a water demon... The Niffler is back. Pickett is back. It's been brilliant to be part of creating those

originally, and now we get to do them again and try to do everything better. There are fewer beasts this time, but where they do feature, they feature more prominently. In a sense, one of the biggest beasts is actually Paris.'

In all that they do, Manz and his team constantly think about the beasts in relation to their environment. How does a Matagot patrol the floors of the Ministère des Affaires Magiques de la France? Once the Zouwu has escaped from the circus, how will she cope with the streets of Paris?

'We don't want the beasts to be designed in isolation,' says Heyman. Each one needs to be an individual character and an integrated part of the world.

Introduced as one of the animals captured by Skender and cruelly displayed at Circus Arcanus, the Zouwu is a good case in point. The biggest creature in the film, she is described as a large feline beast – as big as an elephant – with four fangs and long sharp claws. Furthermore, she has a long multicoloured tail.

The irony is that even though she is terrifying to behold, she is a timid thing. When we first meet her she is depressed because

Opposite: Final film stills of the Zouwu *(above)* and Augurey *(below). This page (top to bottom):* concept art of the Matagot by Ken Barthelmey; concept art of the Kappa by Scott McInnes.

of Skender's mistreatment. Newt will help her rediscover her old self.

The visual effects team like to do their own research, following the description in the screenplay back to the mythical creatures of French and, in this case, Chinese literature. Those descriptions were then sent to the concept artists, who returned with a host of different Zouwus. These were then whittled down to a few, which were put in front of Yates to see which one he reacted to best — always a telling moment.

'That then got honed down and honed down,' says Manz. It took fifty different concepts to harness an essential 'Zouwuness', before a 3D version was built in the computer for Yates to see it brought to life.

'They are the other actors in the film,' says Manz, and it is with these rough animations that they begin to discover how they behave. 'Then we've got puppeteers on set to stand in for the creatures when we're filming and we learn from that. It's a journey of months and years.'

These puppet versions range from a tennis ball on a stick for the correct eye-line, right up to full-sized models that imitate the beast. There was a beanbag version of the Niffler, and tiny stick puppets of Pickett, the Bowtruckle, that still required two separate puppeteers to operate, one for the arms and one for the legs.

Bohanna estimates they have done more puppeteering on this film than the last. With puppeteer Robin Guiver, who worked on the lauded stage version of *War Horse*, spearheading the on-set performance of the beasts. 'The lovely thing about what Robin does is he puts a lot of characterization into his interaction with the actors. That helps guide the animators.'

Once again, Eddie Redmayne was thrilled at the opportunity to get up close and personal with the creatures and figure out his own way of communicating with them. Through this, he gets the chance to offer his own ideas to the mix. 'It's really a team effort,' he says. 'This entire sort of concoction of puppeteers, stunt specialists, movement coaches, visual effects guys, and an actor.'

For the Zouwu, Pierre Bohanna's prop making department built an extraordinary puppet for Redmayne to attempt to tame. 'It had three or four men dressed in full-on green suits moving it around,' the actor says, laughing at what has become just another part of his working day. 'And at the front was an actual sculpted head.'

'She's almost like a Chinese dragon puppet,' says Bohanna. 'So we made a head for her. She has this incredible dreadlocked hair. There was a point where she cuddles Newt, so we made a soft foam version, with the puppeteers essentially wrapping themselves around Eddie, with his head sticking out.'

EVEN MORE FANTASTIC BEASTS

'There are no strange creatures,' declares Newt Scamander, setting out his firmly held belief in the second Fantastic Beasts film, 'only blinkered people...' The Magizoologist will certainly have the chance to prove his point. As the title of the franchise still makes clear, Newt will encounter a host of fascinating new fauna alongside some familiar friends. Most of which will prove more misunderstood than fearsome.

Found in Newt's basement hospital, the magical Circus Arcanus, the Ministère des Affaires Magiques de la France, and in one case loose on the streets of Paris, the new film will feature a wild collection of different beasts.

Thankfully, for his new mission, Newt has managed to fix the lock on his case. 'Well, he's got it under control a bit,' laughs prop modeller Pierre Bohanna, who has updated the case ready for the Magizoologist's trip to Paris. His portable menagerie will once again come in handy.

'We've got new beasts, beasts from all sorts of places,' says producer David Heyman. Here is a handy guide to those beasts to look out for in The Crimes of Grindelwald.

AUGUREY

(Newt's basement): large, owl-like bird with sharp talons, a horned beak and an expressive face. On its head the Augurey has long, individual tendrils that feather out at the ends. Its long tail feathers are dark green and interspersed with pretty purple and green plumes.

BOGGART

(Hogwarts): a shapeshifting, non-being that instantaneously takes on the appearance of an observer's worst fear. Tellingly, the young Newt as a student at Hogwarts will see his Boggart as a desk at the Ministry.

BOWTRUCKLE

(Newt's basement and Paris): the diminutive, sprig-like beast has a complex social life, and only nests in trees made of wand-quality wood. Newt has a special attachment to a Bowtruckle named Pickett, who is still often to be found in Newt's breast pocket.

CHUPACABRA

(New York): this blood-sucking creature has six legs, spines and a vicious-looking set of teeth.

FIREDRAKE

(Circus Arcanus): looks like a small flying lizard with long antennae. It could be mistaken for a dragon, except, instead of breathing fire, the Firedrake emits sparks from the end of its tail that set anything flammable ablaze.

HINKYPUNK

(Paris): useful in disrupting tracking charms, Newt carries a Hinkypunk in a lantern as he travels to Paris. Resembling a glowing, one-legged tuft of smoke, not unlike a Will-'O-the-wisp, care must be taken with these impish varmints, who don't take well to being confined in a lantern. On set, the Hinkypunk was created using a light in a jar over which the visual effects team will animate the ethereal creature.

KAPPA

(Circus Arcanus): a Japanese water spirit rather like a monkey, with scales instead of fur, as well as a taste for human blood.

KELPIE

(Newt's basement): a creature that lives underwater, where its camouflage is looking like long, thick strands of green kelp. The Kelpie is extremely strong and hard to tame and has a nasty bite. However, once bridled, it is docile and, for those who know how to handle it, the Kelpie can provide a fast underwater ride.

For the shoot, an accurate, full-scale Kelpie model was made with a realistic head and shoulder for Eddie Redmayne to ride on. This was then placed onto a trolley and pushed around the set. Puppeteers operated the head, while Redmayne hung on for dear life so that the visual effects team could gain an accurate position for Newt.

LEUCROTTA

(Newt's basement): similar to a stocky reindeer, only with a gigantic mane and a mouth the size of a dustbin lid.

MATAGOT

(Ministère des Affaires Magiques de la France): the feline Matagot is a spirit familiar somewhat resembling a hairless Sphinx cat. In France, they are utilized by the Ministry of Magic to do menial jobs, including staffing the mailroom and providing security for various other departments. Matagots won't attack unless provoked, but then will transform into something far more menacing.

MOONCALF

(Newt's basement): the Magizoologist is looking after a whole family of these shy, moon-obsessed quadrupeds with large webbed feet and bulging eyes.

NIFFLER

(Newt's basement and Paris): our small furry friend is a cross between a duck-billed platypus and a mole. With an irrepressible predilection for anything glittery, this remarkably fast and agile little beast will snatch or steal whatever shiny object catches its eye and store its treasures in the pouch on its belly. They do not make good house pets.

BABY NIFFLERS

(Newt's basement): Nifflers can have large litters of up to eight babies, which can come in a variety of colours: ranging from typical black to brown and white, grey & white, and tricolour. They are born with an instinctive penchant for anything shiny, and pound-for-pound are just as mischievous as their parents.

ONI

(Circus Arcanus): a large pot-bellied Japanese beast with warthog-like tusks. They grow to the size of a room.

THESTRAL

(New York): a skeletal but strong-winged beast that has some equine traits but is decidedly not a horse, with long bat-like wings, forked hooves and a pointed tail. Thestrals appear black in colour to those who can see them; however, they are only visible to those who have witnessed death firsthand.

ZOUWU

(Circus Arcanus and Paris): a monstrously large feline beast – as big as an elephant – with a striped body, scraggly mane, four fangs that curl up out of its mouth, and long sharp claws. Perhaps its most distinctive feature is its disproportionately long and ruffled multicoloured tail. Native to China, Zouwus are incredibly powerful and fast, capable of travelling 1,000 miles in a day. The Zouwu in *Fantastic Beasts: The Crimes of Grindelwald* was captured by Skender, the owner and Ringmaster of the wizarding world's Circus Arcanus, and bears the scars of its abuse.

HOGWARTS

RETURNING To HOGWARTS

BACK TO SCHOOL

One of the most exciting developments in the second *Fantastic Beasts* film is also one of the most familiar. For the sequel will return to the classrooms and corridors where Harry, Hermione and Ron once ran amok. Or to be exact, *will* run amok in seventy years' time. For the filmmakers, it has been the challenge of going back to Hogwarts School of Witchcraft and Wizardry before it was the Hogwarts we know and love.

With the second film, J.K. Rowling is deliberately drawing the two franchises closer together. 'We meet ancestors and relatives of characters in the *Beasts* movies who are seen in the Potter books,' she explains. 'I don't want to give too much away, but you stumble across quite a few people and places and things that you'll recognize.'

At the same time, this remains a clever balancing act. 'I'm telling a discrete story within the *Fantastic Beasts* franchise that is only hinted at in the Potter books,' she says, 'which is the rise of Grindelwald, who was a wizard who seriously threatened the security of the wizarding and the larger world, and his antagonist, Dumbledore, who of course is a key character in the Potter books. This was backstory that I always had lots of ideas about, and now I get to tell it, which is artistically really satisfying.'

Standing beneath a skeleton, Jude Law is filmed teaching his blue-robed students in the Defence Against the Dark Arts classroom.

While such memorable locations as the Great Hall and the Gryffindor Common Room are yet to take a bow, we will still get a thrilling insight into Hogwarts circa 1927.

'It is an ancient building, which you might think wouldn't change that much,' says production designer Stuart Craig, who has spent a good portion of his career imagining and reimagining the great Scottish castle. 'The thing is, on Harry Potter, because we started with only two books with the rest of them unwritten at that stage, by necessity things kept changing.'

Harry Potter and the Prisoner of Azkaban had required an astronomy tower where one hadn't existed in the first two films. 'So without any respect for continuity we changed things,' he laughs. 'One of the things we changed most was the way into Hogwarts. In the final movie, for the great battle, we put in a causeway that leads to the front entrance. We will see that causeway in this movie.'

Overall, they have played on the familiarity of the famous architecture, flashing-forward to the school to come. In some respects, it has been just like old times.

'I never thought we'd be getting the old model out, but we have,' says visual effects supervisor Tim Burke, referring to the finely detailed miniature of Hogwarts that they have kept in storage. 'We have restored all the old Hogwarts models, and even went back and shot some plates in Scotland.'

'It is also very obvious in the wizarding equipment,' notes Craig: 'Quidditch and cauldrons, owls and owl cages. It's fun to see early versions of that.'

The graphic design team have created a set of new-old books, including a slightly redesigned Hogwarts exercise book. 'I think fans will like that it is so familiar, like the ones we had in Harry Potter,' says Eduardo Lima. 'All the crests for the houses remained the same.'

The production also returned to shoot at Lacock Abbey in Wiltshire, whose lovely mid-sixteenth-century cloisters with vaulted ceilings have become a signature of Hogwarts.

'We are slowly drawing back into the magical world we've seen before,' explains construction manager Paul Hayes, admitting he would have loved to have built even more. 'We built the Defence Against the Dark Arts classroom, which was lovely because the original set from the Harry Potter films had never made it to storage and had fallen apart. That was the one set I couldn't save.'

DUMBLEDORE'S CLASSROOM

Long before becoming headmaster, Albus Dumbledore was the master of Defence Against the Dark Arts, and the new film will give us a chance to see how the most famous of Hogwarts's many classrooms once reflected his personality.

In terms of layout it was identical. 'We had the original drawings,' says Hayes. 'I even went back to Ashridge House to copy the exact stone mould we used before so we would have the correct stone for the classroom.'

'Everything was oak beams and rafters,' adds Craig. 'I guess it doesn't change much in seventy years.'

For set decorator Anna Pinnock it was a case of maintaining a philosophy of making it look the same but different. 'You are always battling,' she says. 'You want to keep the connection that people love, and still do something new.'

Like Hayes, Pinnock delved into the Harry Potter archives. 'We had some furniture available from the original films. I tried to replicate the feel of the original classroom and then have Dumbledore's presence bring something new.'

Over the Harry Potter saga, a recurring motif was that every new teacher of the Dark Arts populated the classroom with items to help them teach the class, as well as a few more personal knick-knacks: Remus Lupin had his bone and fossil collecting pieces, vain Gilderoy Lockhart his own books, while Dolores Umbridge had nothing at all — in line with her flat denial of Voldemort's return.

With Dumbledore in charge, they could hint toward the treasure trove within the headmaster's office to come. 'He's into astrology and astronomy in a big way,' says prop modeller Pierre Bohanna, who actually pulled out some of the original clockwork pieces from Warner Bros. Studio Tour Leavesden.

They also set about adding to his collection

Opposite (top to bottom): Aurors Apparate on to the footbridge; prop of the Defence Against the Dark Arts text book; young Leta (Thea Lamb). *Top to bottom:* Hogwarts students get ready to leave, taking their owls and cases; Dumbledore in his classroom with a giant microscope *(inset)* prop of ornamental puzzle ball found on Dumbledore's desk.

Top to bottom: David Yates
enjoys the applause of his
enthusiastic young cast; props
of textbooks in the four House
colours; filming Hogwarts
exteriors at Lacock Abbey.
Opposite, top to bottom: a young
Newt (Joshua Shea) and Leta
(Thea Lamb) form a friendship
under the stairs at Hogwarts;
Jude Law is filmed in front
of the Mirror of Erised; the
Mirror reveals to Dumbledore
himself with Grindelwald.

of arcane whirligigs and globes. Bohanna joined Pinnock on a research trip to the Oxford and London Science Museums, seeking inspiration from historical apparatus. 'In Oxford there were several pieces we liked,' recalls Bohanna. 'One was a model of the Moon that was set within these brass gyroscopic rigs. But because it was from the 1830s, it only had the map of one side of the Moon.'

It was exactly the kind of prop-making experience Bohanna adores, with 'lots of crystals, lens stands and the sorts of equipment relating to astronomy.' They even found a microscope that would ironically make a fantastic telescope, and

they made a 'lovely' twelve-foot high version that sits resplendently in the corner of the classroom.

When it came to Dumbledore's pupils and their Hogwarts uniforms, the costume department had the added complication of not only returning to 1927 Hogwarts, but flashing back to an even earlier era, where the young Newt and his classmates attempt to negotiate a Boggart under Dumbledore's tutelage.

'We had a couple different time periods,' says Colleen Atwood, but was surprised how little variation there was in school uniforms right through to the nineties of Harry Potter's time.

'We did use the Harry Potter costumes as a starting point, even though this is now a different period,' explains costume supervisor Charlotte Finlay. They still have all four house colours, badges, and ties: all the motifs that fans will recognise, but there is one significant change.

'The difference is that the robes for Harry Potter were black and the newly designed robes are dark blue,' says Finlay. 'We still have the hoods that represent each House, but the cut has been slightly redesigned for the period.'

NEWT'S SANCTUARY

During the flashback to Newt's unsettled schooldays, we get a glimpse of his formative ventures into Magizoology, for which was built a small but significant set. Stocked with a collection of snail-like Streelers, a tadpole tank, and an injured baby raven, which he is tending, Newt has established his first sanctuary for beasts in a secret cupboard space at Hogwarts. It is a forerunner of the case and basement he will design as an adult.

In a typically quirky Stuart Craig-like touch, the production designer had imagined this strange, cramped refuge hidden in between the vaulted ceiling of the cloisters and the floor above. 'Newt's little secret menagerie is in that space,' he explains. 'You walk through a small door off the cloister, go immediately up this tight little stone staircase, and end up sitting on the vaulting of the cloister below.'

Adds Craig, 'I'm not sure if people will quite work that out, but it has the right atmosphere and it's interesting photographically.'

For Redmayne this space provided another keen insight into Newt's psychology. 'He felt much more comfortable in there with them than he did with other students. Right from when he was a kid at Hogwarts, he would go and collect damaged creatures and look after them and revitalize them. It was something in his blood.'

Meet the young
ALBUS DUMBLEDORE

What was Dumbledore like in his prime? Back when he merely taught Defence Against the Dark Arts at Hogwarts. Did he still speak in riddles? Did he meddle and plot, working to an enigmatic agenda? Was he kind and witty? Did he have a beard? Above all, could the actor make the role his own, stepping out from under the shadow of both Richard Harris and Michael Gambon?

Arguably, the most fascinating challenge J.K. Rowling presented to the next instalment of *Fantastic Beasts* was the introduction of the iconic headmaster seventy years younger than when we last set eyes on him.

'We meet Dumbledore as a man in, I would say, early middle age,' says Rowling. 'So, he's a youthful man, but he's an adult. The Dumbledore we meet here is clever, is gifted, but he's mysterious. We see him through the eyes of Newt Scamander, who is a man apart from politics, and we learn that he was a great teacher, but he's a man who doesn't appear to tell anyone the whole truth. He's a man who is burdened with knowledge. You know, it's not easy being Dumbledore. He often has information he can't share – he is often swimming against the crowd.'

The Dumbledore in this film is not really the Dumbledore we met in the Harry Potter films. 'His relationship with Harry is different to his relationship with Newt,' says producer David Heyman. 'Harry was much more in awe and respectful of Dumbledore. Newt is respectful but less in awe. He is aware of being manipulated by him, and is less tolerant of it.'

Finding the right man to fill such wizarding boots was a tall order. 'There are so many qualities that we had to find,' says Heyman. 'You want that wisdom. You want the wit. You want someone who has these demons. You are looking for the cleverest man in the room, someone with absolute authority. Someone who has a physicality, a sexuality, a maturity, and who can stand face to face with Johnny Depp and with Eddie Redmayne and not be acted off the screen.'

Luckily for them, that person had already applied for the job.

Jude Law was already well versed in Harry Potter. He had read the books to his children, listened to Stephen Fry's 'wonderful recordings' on long, family journeys; and they had religiously taken in the films.

The celebrated, London-born star of *The Talented Mr. Ripley*, *Cold Mountain* and the *Sherlock Holmes* movies, an actor who has collaborated with greats like Clint Eastwood, Steven Spielberg and Martin Scorsese, had been so taken with the first *Fantastic Beasts* film he thought he really ought to look into being in the next one.

So he made his own enquiries. Where else is this going to go? Are they looking to bring in any of the old characters? Planting the idea with Messrs Rowling, Heyman and Yates.

'Whether that stoked any curiosity from their part I don't know,' he says. 'But I got a call early on

saying they were looking to cast a young Dumbledore. It was a very good day when I got the phone call saying they wanted me to play him.'

You may recall from the myriad revelations at the end of the Harry Potter saga that Dumbledore and Gellert Grindelwald had once been close. As young, idealistic men, they had made plans to unearth the powerful Deathly Hallows artifacts and overthrow the existing order of wizards. In its place, they would create a brave new world where witches and wizards need not hide in the shadows but would reign over Muggles for the good of all. Tragedy tore them apart, leaving Grindelwald to pervert their flawed dreams to his own ends, and Dumbledore to carry a great responsibility toward the past.

'The relationship between Grindelwald and Dumbledore is key to making Dumbledore

Dumbledore,' says Rowling. 'They met when they were very young, late teens, and they are both outstanding wizards. I mean, spectacularly gifted. In this movie, you're just getting a taste of what their relationship is and what it will be.'

'There is so much going on beneath the surface,' says Law, who has spent long afternoons in the company of J.K. Rowling as she helped him harness the complexities of the wizard. 'Here is someone who has been told since being an infant that he was special. That he had the capability of being very powerful. But just at the wrong time he went through a crushing personal drama. His father is imprisoned. Then there is the death of his mother, which leads to the death of his sister. He is dealing with deep, harrowing wounds.'

His 'emotional intimacy' blinded him to Grindelwald's darker leanings, and eventually led to

Top to bottom:
Dumbledore instructs young Newt; blackboard instructions on Transformation; *(inset)* final prop of a 1920s broomstick. *Opposite, top to bottom:* Leta traces where she carved her and Newt's initials in her desk lid; Jude and Eddie relax on set; Dumbledore receives an unwelcome visit from the Ministry. *Inset:* The enigmatic Albus Dumbledore.

a heart-rending confrontation with his great friend, and yet another scar.

With his heart 'packed with ice', the actor suggests, it is little wonder that he struggles to trust other people, which in turn has led to so much secrecy.

'He also has a sense that he can put things right,' he explains. 'That with the right application, whether it is through study, or spreading the good word through his pupils, or indeed his machinations behind the scenes, he can rectify the wrongs that he's been a part of creating.'

Hogwarts has become a kind of sanctuary for the wizard.

'There's a sea of complexities there,' the actor continues. 'But shimmering under the surface is someone who is impish and cheeky and curious and anarchic and brilliant.

Thanks to a self-imposed exile, he has to use his relationships with similarly motivated and morally grounded wizards to try and halt the rise of Grindelwald.

'Newt, he knows, is someone who has a very strong moral compass,' says Law. 'Unfortunately, Dumbledore is somebody who operates three steps ahead of everyone else. You could accuse him of, not necessarily manipulating, but leading people into doing things they don't particularly want to do.'

At Dumbledore's insistence,

with a typically dramatic flourish during a rendezvous atop the roof of St Paul's Cathedral, Newt reluctantly agrees to go undercover to Paris and track down Credence.

There is the hint that, when he is ready, Dumbledore will step forward and confront his friend-turned-nemesis. For now, it is best he works in the shadows. Law can see that he did the same thing with Harry Potter. 'He lets people know just enough, and not have the burden of seeing everything too soon.'

Together with Rowling and director David Yates, Law has spent a lot of time considering Dumbledore

in physical terms. How did he walk and talk as a younger man? How much did he laugh? How did he present himself to his class? He was a bit of dandy, he learned. A man who enjoyed a certain flair to his dress sense.

'We looked at wonderful pictures of philosophers and artists of that period, who wore suits with a certain panache,' elaborates Law. 'We loved the idea of giving him the eccentricity of a professor, and the beard was important because Jo referenced it in the script. But that makes him somewhat unusual in this period, because not that many men wore beards. He is this slightly flamboyant bookworm.'

Perhaps most fascinating of all to fans will be the opportunity to see Dumbledore in the familiar embrace of a Hogwarts classroom. We will see him as a popular master of the often ill-fated Defence Against the Dark Arts curriculum, tutoring his wide-eyed pupils in the art of tackling a Boggart.

'It was really wonderful,' recalls Law: 'the children in that scene were so thrilled to be there, and David constructed the filming so that it really felt like a class. My parents are both teachers, so I drew from that. Although it was a slightly out-of-body experience to be doing so at Hogwarts.'

While this might be the younger, finely tailored variation on the mighty wizard, it was still important to plant the seeds of the Dumbledore to come. Even before he had read the script, it was made clear to Law that he was starting on a journey in which we would learn how Dumbledore became the great wizard we see in the Harry Potter stories.

He laughs. 'I initially thought I was going to steer clear of watching either Harris or Gambon. But I couldn't resist. It was such an obvious opportunity to watch all the films again, which was such fun. But I also just wanted to see if there was anything I could eke from them, even though it was important to all of us that we weren't creating *that* Dumbledore. We were creating the man who was going to *become* that Dumbledore.'

COLLEEN ATWOOD ON ALBUS DUMBLEDORE

Given we meet the professor in his younger days, his look is a long way from the flowing robes and wilting hat of the Harry Potter films. 'He is dressed in soft tweed fabrics and a heavy corduroy coat,' says Atwood, 'there is an approachable feel to him: he is popular with the students, a nurturing teacher.'

Nevertheless, with the colours, a sort of puce and a hint of purple, there is the slightest suggestion of the grand figure to come. 'It's sort of the same depth of colour as his costume is in the Harry Potter series,' notes Atwood. 'Nothing too obvious.'

The enigmatic case of
LETA LESTRANGE

Both stunning and inscrutable, Leta Lestrange cuts a striking figure across the new adventures of Newt Scamander. While establishing herself at the Ministry of Magic, she is a paragon of style amongst London's witches of 1927. In other words, she is effortlessly glamorous. Stepping into those fashionable shoes is actress, singer, and model Zoë Kravitz, offspring of rock royalty in father Lenny Kravitz.

Like all of J.K. Rowling's creations, there is far more to Leta beneath the impeccable surface. The Lestrange family are pure-bloods, those families or individuals who are without Muggle blood. If the family name sounds familiar, among Leta's less convivial descendants (by marriage) is Bellatrix Lestrange, who will wreak such havoc in the Harry Potter films.

'When we meet her we feel that she's a woman who's struggling to emerge into the light, but she's burdened by her past,' says the author. 'Her family casts this enormous shadow over her. At this point in wizarding history, the Lestranges are the very epitome of pure-blood aristocracy.'

Given we would get a look at Leta in a photograph in Newt's shed — where Queenie quickly divines that Leta is a 'taker' — Kravitz actually had to audition for the sequel even before the first movie came out. She admits she had very little to go on.

She had an idea of Leta's legacy from Bellatrix, and it helped that Helena Bonham Carter, is one of Kravitz's favourite actresses. So she knew where the family *goes*, and some idea of what it means to be a pure-blood. She also established that there was a history between Leta and Newt. But that was it. As she got closer to getting the role, she had the chance to read with Eddie Redmayne.

'He put the pieces together for me,' she says. 'Though, at that point, I don't think anyone, other than Jo, really knew where Leta was going story-wise. But he did his best.'

Born in Venice, California, Kravitz took her first steps on her acting career in 2007 with culinary comedy *No Reservations*, and has swiftly risen to roles in a host of blockbusters: *X-Men: First Class* (as Angele Salvatore, with the superhuman ability to fly), the *Divergent* films, science fiction adventure *After Earth*, and dystopian action classic *Mad Max: Fury Road*. With the Californian domestic tribulations of television series *Big Little Lies* proving she was equally at home in reality.

Kravitz has thoroughly embraced being a witch. Despite being unfamiliar with the Harry Potter books as a youngster, she was still very into magic and has had a ball casting spells. 'Sometimes it feels as if we are really accessing magic, as everyone is so

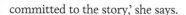

committed to the story,' she says.

While Leta is no angel, she isn't necessarily evil. Conflicted is a better way of describing her. Given she's a Lestrange, producer David Heyman expects there to be an automatic assumption that Leta is not to be trusted.

'The Lestrange family name comes with a whole raft of expectations and associations,' he says, 'so she has to live with that, and she certainly has a dark side. She has done bad things in the past. But that does not necessarily define her. She's someone who is decent. She and Theseus, Newt's brother, are a couple. But she is wrestling with what is expected of her and who she really is.'

'She's quite complicated,' says director David Yates, 'a little damaged, and confused... She's kind of a tragic figure in a way.'

Back in their Hogwarts days, when only teenagers, Leta and Newt developed a special bond. Both outsiders in their own way, they were instinctually drawn to one another.

'Their oddness brings them together,' explains Kravitz. 'On paper it might not make any sense, but Newt is such a compassionate person who loves beasts. He loves things that no one else will love, and Leta is that in a lot of ways.'

The legacy of their friendship will be the seed of much romantic confusion in the second film. Before it even begins, Leta has become engaged to Newt's older brother Theseus. Nevertheless, it could be that Newt still understands Leta a lot better than his brother does.

'Leta lives in a place, emotionally, where no one wants to be,' says Kravitz, who admits that has been tough to play. 'She has a lot of self-loathing. I had to find that in myself — the things I don't like about myself. Dipping in and out of that has been quite intense.'

Leta is also in possession of a secret regarding her own family, a secret that links mysteriously to Credence's quest to know his true identity and place in the world.

'It is something that unravels during the course of the film,' says Yates, 'and that's always a very interesting thing to investigate — guilt and what it does to you. Her journey goes to a lot of interesting, odd, intense places.'

COLLEEN ATWOOD ON LETA LESTRANGE

'She needed something of an old-European, aristocratic hauteur compared to the American witches,' says Atwood. 'She has a certain decadence and glamour that comes reflected in the rich materials of her costume. It wasn't something she had to seek out. She was the real deal. Plus, Zoë Kravitz can pull off *anything*. She's the perfect kind of person to dress.'

STUART CRAIG · PRODUCTION DESIGN

Stuart Craig puts his role in simple terms — he supplies the background. This can involve choice of location, the designing and building of scenery and sets, and working in collaboration with the visual effects department, who extend his sets to the horizon. 'Giving it the widest possible context,' he says.

In other words, he turns J.K. Rowling's flights of imagination into three solid dimensions. In truth, the seventy-five-year-old, award-winning British veteran, who served as production designer on every Harry Potter film, is largely responsible for how we picture the wizarding world. The secret, he says, is not to consider it magic.

'Over the years, we've worked out something very simple, which is that we try to make things look absolutely real, and the magic comes from that. Then it comes as a surprise and is all the more effective. We don't try and build fantasy sets. We try to let fantasy be born somehow out of the sets.'

Modest to a fault, Craig is an eloquent and fascinating authority on the warp and weft of this world. Before he made his acquaintance with the boy wizard and his remarkable creator, he had won Oscars for *Ghandi*, *Dangerous Liaisons* and *The English Patient*. And such is Rowling's respect for his being a specialist on her creation, she insists he approve all the theme park attractions based on her books.

With the change of period and variety of settings, the Fantastic Beasts films have presented fresh challenges. With the sky-scraping modernism of New York, the first *Fantastic Beasts* had actually felt more modern than Harry Potter,

Cast and crew are dwarfed by the grandeur of Craig's vision for Newt's basement.

which was largely stationed in its Gothic school. The sequel mixes that sense of progress with the gravity and history of London and Paris in 1927. The story has also expanded its horizons.

'It is a development,' says Craig. 'The story of the two couples continues, but is quite dramatically changed. Also the bigger story, the story of Grindelwald and potentially this war of the worlds that he is trying to start is a major development from that brief glimpse we had at the end of the last movie.'

Whatever Rowling conceives on the page will be given a touch of Craig's magic before it reaches the screen. He provides many of the little left field touches that make it so much more than a work of fantasy. A task that stretches from months of concept design and preproduction, right through to postproduction, where he checks in with the

visual effects teams to ensure the set extensions are 'compatible with the foregrounds' and the architectural design he has laid out.

'Stuart is a genius without a doubt,' says construction manager Paul Hayes. 'His vision is second to none. He'll sit down and do a little sketch, sometimes only a pencil sketch that he'll hand to me, and we'll work our way back from that.'

'We're trying to keep as much in camera as possible,' says art director Martin Foley. 'Stuart will always design the whole thing, and then we will pare it back to what's cost effective. But Stuart is always pushing boundaries. Four-walled sets is a given; it makes it easier for shooting as you can turn the camera around and look the other way.'

In turn, Craig says that Rowling it still capable of surprising him. At the beginning of this movie, for instance, she introduces Dumbledore

Above: Craig takes J.K.Rowling on a tour through the streets of their vision of Paris.

on the rooftop of St Paul's. 'That is a pretty arresting image,' he appreciates.

With the Fantastic Beasts films based on original screenplays rather than adapted from the fixtures of pre-existing books, there is far more collaboration between writer, designer and director. Rowling is a frequent visitor to the art department, where they have mounted a permanent exhibition of research material, including concept sketches that evolve as the script develops.

'These images are in story order, and you can see the juxtaposition of certain things,' explains Craig. 'Jo witnesses all of that, and she is carried along with it as we are carried along by her instructions, too.'

Did he ever think he would be immersed in her world for seventeen years? He laughs. 'No idea, but it has been amazing the way it turned out. It has been so satisfying to take something and keep adding to it. It's a privilege that movie designers don't normally have.'

Moreover, he has to keep in mind that there are three further Newt Scamander adventures yet to come. 'Yes, it is a real issue,' he says. 'There have been instances, where David Yates or David Heyman will say to Jo, "We are about to get rid of this, is there any reason why we shouldn't?" And so the question is asked. Jo obviously has drafted it out. You couldn't embark on all of this unless you knew the end.'

Like us, he is eager to know where they might be headed next. 'For me, this journey through architectural history is an absolutely spectacular gift, it couldn't be more interesting.'

COLLEEN ATWOOD · COSTUME DESIGN

Legendary costume designer Colleen Atwood admits it was a strange feeling returning to the world of *Fantastic Beasts* having won an Oscar for the first film. It had been a wonderful honour, of course, but all she could think about was what lay ahead. Even after her fourth Academy Award from twelve nominations (dating all the way back to *Little Women* in 1995), she explains in her inimitably, straight-talking style, with every new film you have to 'up your game.'

And J.K. Rowling had naturally given her a set of fascinating new challenges.

The second film spreads a far wider net than the first: it darts from New York to London to Paris, including three separate Ministries of Magic, an entire Parisian couture, an unappetizing circus, a near-immortal alchemist, and a brief return to Hogwarts including Professor Dumbledore in his stylish, Jude Law-shaped pomp. History was on the march, with fashion at its vanguard. Moreover, each of the main characters was evolving and deepening, requiring a rethink in terms of their costume.

'There were definitely some curveballs,' explains Atwood. 'Paris is a little more glamorous, and we have street shoots, big clothing scenes. There is much more of a connection to the Potter world. Plus, there is a huge influx of new personalities into the story. It was like starting a whole new movie.'

Overall, the feel was slightly moodier, with a sense of impending darkness. 'You feel the shadow of evil,' she says. 'There is fog. There's a lot of atmosphere in the film: more night work, more of a dramatic slant.'

With over seventy films to her name, nothing can faze the Seattle-born Atwood. She is a miracle of multi-tasking. While

Opposite: Dumbledore was dressed in soft tweed to make him appear approachable. *Inset:* Circus Arcanus ringmaster Skender is dressed to impress.

answering the call of the second Fantastic Beasts film, she was simultaneously designing costumes for long-time collaborator Tim Burton's reimagining of *Dumbo*, as well as a new adaptation of the video game *Tomb Raider*. She still takes great delight in the opportunity for 'exploration' that her calling offers.

Atwood's starting point with any new film is twofold: breaking down the script into constituent requirements (simply: what costumes are needed) and a conversation with the director about how he or she sees the world. 'Then I go see what the art department's doing. What world are they conceptualizing?'

Rowling, she says, will occasionally pay a visit, comment on a few things, and then she's gone. 'It's like she's magically there and then she isn't.' The costume designer is clearly impressed. 'She is a very dynamic woman — she comes in for the big moments and then goes and probably figures out the next one.'

Focusing on the era in question, Atwood researches photographs of people in different environments, waiting for the trigger of inspiration. Fortunately, she knew a researcher in New York who happened to be French and was very familiar with the history of Paris, which would dominate the new film.

There is no need to slavishly stick to the year in question. Some people might still be 'feeling their own time', which could be ten years before, whereas others might be 'feeling the future'. The film might be set in 1927, but many of her designs are already merging with the thirties.

In terms of location, London had that thriller vibe. What David Yates called a 'nod toward film noir.' Atwood looked at 1949 classic *The Third Man*. 'Plus, I focused a lot on silhouette,' she says. 'Especially when you're

in this foggy, lower light, the silhouette of a costume is really important.'

Silhouettes are key to costume design. You need a variety of different shapes in a scene. 'Otherwise, it could get very generic,' says Atwood. 'You are trying to communicate character.' Magical types have what she calls, 'a stronger silhouette'.

Paris in the twenties offered what she terms 'a little more modernism' than you get in London. 'You know, mentally.' With New York in the last film, it was the height of the twenties, the flapper era, which was instantly recognizable. In Paris, the skirts are that bit longer, dresses have stronger lines, and the silhouettes are much more fitted.

'It's a little bit more sensual on the outside than the earlier period,' says Atwood. 'It's Paris, so I can get away with a little bit of something here.'

Meanwhile, the men's clothes are slightly more tailored, the trousers a bit wider. 'There's just little, subtle differences, but they make for a little more flow and movement, and a squarer shoulder.'

The 'gritty combination' of magical settings and social classes on display in the city has required Atwood to look at the sexy, musical Parisian underworld as well as the upmarket side. For example, the rundown Circus Arcanus, which Atwood defines as a 'night circus' and a long way from the elaborate big tops she dressed in Tim Burton movies such as *Big Fish*.

Like every principal location, Paris also came with its own colour palette, where costumes are designed to accent colour such as the red in shop awnings and vice versa. As with silhouettes, colour is another crucial ingredient in Atwood's process.

'I do feel the colour of the characters as I'm thinking about them. It's hard to describe, but especially with the four main characters, who often share the same frame, you want to make sure they aren't fighting each other visually.'

Overall, she has been trying to 'step away from

Above: Queenie and Jacob stand out in the crowd. *Opposite:* Atwood discusses one of her dress costumes with David Yates. *Inset:* Claudia Kim in full costume as the Maledictus.

Atwood, who estimates five thousand costumes have been produced, bought or hired for the film. Meantime, the weathering department is frantically adding holes, letting the washing machine batter her lovely fabrics into submission, and then bleaching and painting on top of them. All in order to give that lived-in and used-up quality that Yates is looking for. It may be a new film but nothing can feel new.

Once production is underway, Atwood's day is spent jumping back and forth between the set and her workshop, where new costumes are being established. It's a cycle she is well used to, but finds thrilling nonetheless. Each film, she says, has its unique pleasures. Of particular delight in this one has been the chance to focus on headwear. The wizarding sophisticates of Paris have a predilection for hats.

'Everyone pretty much wore a hat in this era,' explains Atwood. 'I have flat caps with little snap-brims that were common with the working class. Then there's the Fedora, which is the gentleman's hat of the period, which has a fairly high crown, but not too big a brim — that came in the forties. Jude's hat is a little bit of a nod toward a Trilby.'

As we saw in the first *Fantastic Beasts*, ladies millinery of the twenties tended toward the cloche, which comes down and cover up most of the hair. So Atwood has pushed it into the thirties, for the 'sculptural aspect' of classic movies. French Aurors have berets, which was kind of a cliché, she remarks, 'but looked really good'. While Grindelwald's acolytes have a really cool look with sharper edges and pointier feathers. 'They definitely have an aspect that is moving into the fascist part of the thirties.'

That echo of reality is vital to her award-lavished work in the Wizarding World. This isn't a magical world you are designing; these are real people who happen to be magical.

black a little bit.' Instead, there are deep, jewel tones for a lot of the magical folk. Dark greens, dark blues. Zoë Kravitz as Leta Lestrange has a dress that is an exquisite moody, deep cherry.

Indeed, Kravitz was in awe of how all Atwood's colours worked in unison. 'When I finally did a scene with a lot of the cast together, I realized how much thought she had put into this. How they are different and why they are different. Colleen is just an artist.'

'It's also for lighting,' says Atwood. 'You need to bring out certain colours, and subdue others.'

The sewing machines of her department begin their chorus roughly four months before shooting. Which Atwood insists is nothing for a film on this scale. With each bespoke costume, she will have a conversation with the actor about how they see their character: 'Sometimes they are very specific about the colour, or the shape, or the direction their costume is moving.' Johnny Depp especially likes to build his character around his dramatic attire.

Atwood will give them a picture of her vision of the film. Not only for their costume, but the world of the film as a whole. Hopefully, for them to get excited about the designs and fabrics she intends to use.

For the store of readymade background costumes, her team has ventured to famous costumiers Tirelli and Peruzzi in Italy and Spain. They have also raided the many flea markets of Paris (and eBay).

'I needed a massive amount of clothes,' says

PARIS

BRINGING PARIS TO LEAVESDEN

ART NOUVEAU

Where the first *Fantastic Beasts* film took Newt Scamander to the glittering metropolis of New York, the second will propel him through the boulevards of Paris. A pattern appears to have been set: with each new adventure, J.K. Rowling will send Newt, his companions, and no doubt a Niffler or two, to explore a new city somewhere in the world. Each setting will give the new film a personality all of its own.

'Harry Potter was rooted in Britain, primarily,' says producer David Heyman. 'It is a pleasure to explore the wizarding world more globally in the Fantastic Beasts series, first in New York and now Paris.'

For Rowling this has been on one of the great glories and joys of the Beasts series. 'It's so freeing to be able to move into these different areas,' she says. 'So, why Paris? It's the nineteen twenties; it had to be Paris. Of course it had to be Paris. In the sexual sense, in the racial sense, the artistic community was far more diverse, in every sense, than you would've met in most other cities in the 1920s. As you enter Paris in the movie, you feel that the membrane between the magical and the mundane worlds is far thinner than it was in New York. The culture is different, both in the Muggle and magical worlds.'

Moreover, for the filmmakers, it was a city that could be recreated on the backlot of Warner Bros. Studios Leavesden, a few miles outside of Watford.

Newt and Jacob meet Yusuf Kama, while surrounded by the complex apparatus of filmmaking.

When Rowling let it be known to Heyman and director David Yates that Paris was their next port of call, they were thrilled. 'Paris of the twenties was a real melting pot of ideas creatively, artistically, socially,' says Yates. 'It was a very vibrant time. It's a magnificent place that has a context for this story.'

There was also an immediate contrast to New York: skyward-bound modernity has been replaced with centuries of history and architecture. Paris was the cream of European cityhood: romantic, classical, and more sinister.

'Our Paris is a little different to the Paris we know today,' says Heyman. 'It hadn't yet been cleaned up, as it was in the eighties. It's a little greyer, but it's still gorgeous, with its wide boulevards, but also secret alleyways. It's still the Paris of boulangeries and patisseries, but it's also magical in its own way.'

The design team took their lead from the expansive city that emerged in the wake of government prefect Georges-Eugène Haussmann's urban renewal at the beginning of the 1850s. 'Haussmann's Paris' as it became known replaced swathes of unsavoury, helter-skelter, medieval districts with the extravagant avenues and squares that came to define the city. Paris doubled in size in a matter of months.

'Those long terraces of elegant, apartment blocks are the hallmark of Haussmann's Paris,' appreciates production designer Stuart Craig. 'Art Nouveau was developed as a style, and that was a potentially very exciting way for us to deliver Paris.'

Art Nouveau was the nineteenth-century movement in architecture and the arts that pursued natural forms. The graceful curving of a branch or a bird's neck were familiar motifs, or glass panels cut to resemble leaves or petals. The style took off in Paris, filtering down into the very street signs, as well as the typography on newspapers and advertising.

'What was really striking about the early Art Nouveau stuff is that

Above: Tracks are carefully laid on to the cobbled street to allow the camera unit to smoothly zoom in on the actors as they walk about the set. *Below:* Graphic prop of a postcard illustrating the attractions of Paris.

everything is hand drawn,' says graphic designer Miraphora Mina. 'That put a little bit of pressure on us in terms of style. Everything was very painterly.'

Several recces to the French capital were required to familiarize themselves with not only the look of the city but its geography.

Rowling had made her own research trips into the Parisian capital, picking out genuine locations and landmarks. The design team found themselves following in her footsteps as if on a treasure hunt, figuring out the exact angle she had been looking from which she was viewing the Sacré Coeur or Rue de Montmorency, but also making their own soundings on what made Paris, well, so Parisian.

They also hired a fulltime researcher in Phil Clark, who over several months established an extensive library of pictures, as well as layouts of interiors and exteriors. 'There is so much material out there,' says Craig, 'it is almost more difficult these days, because the choices are so many and so varied.'

'I was especially taken with the Atget photos,' says set decorator Anna Pinnock, referring to Eugène Atget, the pioneering French photographer of the era. 'I could almost smell the damp and feel the dust!'

Yates had been keen to shoot on location, and they had discussed the possibility quite a long way into the preparation period.

'I think he would have found that a refreshing change,' adds Craig.

Sue Quinn, the location manager, even took a trip to see if Bordeaux could stand in for Paris. But as with the last film and New York, they realized that even though Paris still had extensive terraces of Haussmann apartment blocks, every shop and street is filled with modernity. It would have taken a huge effort to transform

each and every location not only into an authentic 1927 Paris, but its magical alter ego as well.

'The reason we didn't go to Paris was twofold,' says Heyman. 'One, Paris today doesn't look like it did then. We're in 1927: it was much grittier. You still had the residue of pollution all over the buildings. Second, filming at Leavesden gave us so much more control. It gave us the ability to make Paris as we wanted it, not just how it was. And it meant that if the weather was not working in our favour, we could jump on to one of our stages.'

This, Craig accepts, is the chief advantage of building your own European capital. 'It enables everything to be our choice — director and designer. There aren't any of those random, extraneous things that kind of creep in because they are part of an existing location.'

THE LAYOUT

Taking up a significant portion of the 100-acre backlot at Leavesden, which still includes the runway from its former vocation as an aerodrome, Paris was built in the footprint left by New York from the first film. 'As New York streets were also cobbled,' explains Craig, 'it made very good sense to simply sit Paris down on what had been our New York, and use the same cobbled streets.'

The buildings, of course, had to be entirely rebuilt to a height of thirty feet (with visual effects extending them upwards and sideways), but the enormous set still followed the same 800-foot T-shaped layout as New York. 'The crossbar at the top of the T is the more expensive,

Credence and the Maledictus enjoy a quiet moment together on the roof of their hideout, in this concept art by Peter Popken.

upmarket area where the Haussmann-style terraces of apartments are found,' says Craig, noting that this is where Grindelwald occupies an apartment. 'And then the long stem of the T is the poorer districts, or aspects of it are poorer.'

In the lower portion there is a section for the home and studio of Nicolas Flamel, the 600-year-old alchemist. Rowling had specified the Rue de Montmorency, where the real Flamel had lived and reputedly dabbled in arcane science.

For graphic designer Miraphora Mina, it was important to bear in mind that anything you see on the street will likely have been there for twenty years. Which meant taking their research back further in time to the flamboyant styles of the preceding Belle Époque (1871–1914).

The graphic design team had their hands full,

filling up the Morris columns used for street advertising, and the public urinals otherwise known as 'pissoirs', not to say the profusion of shops, bars and restaurants.

'People just went mental with the "look-at-me" ads,' says graphic designer Eduardo Lima. 'Some of the references that we saw, the advertising was huge, covering the sides of buildings.'

A bustling bird market is on the embankment of the (digital) Seine. 'The river is such a big part of Paris,' says Craig: 'the image of the river and the wide towpaths. It is so distinctive. So we put the bird market right there, for no other reason than adding another arresting aspect of Paris.'

Dating back to the early nineteenth century, these open-air Parisian markets offer a rainbow of budgies, canaries, parakeets, and parrots, as

well as chickens and cocks. Each and every bird imprisoned in a garish tableau of cages. The sound of their collective song is both enchanting and heartbreaking; a symbolism that is not lost on Credence.

On a practical level, it presented quite a challenge for set decoration, requiring a large number of real birds.

'It was literally cages and cages with hundreds of birds,' recalls Mina. 'But what they hadn't thought was that all the birds brought in each day were British. And some of these birds can speak. So they're going, "Hello, hello! Good morning, good morning!" In *English*. And we're in Paris! It is one of those things that you don't think of. They'll have to dub in French bird voices: "Bonjour, bonjour! Salut!"'

For all of Haussmann's efforts to bring light and air to the streets, off the beaten track Paris was also still a very un-modernized, nineteenth-century-style city. There was a dark, mysterious atmosphere within its alleyways, staircases and interiors.

'There was a huge variety of interior styles to explore,' she says. 'It was a large canvas that gave us a great deal of freedom in making the subtle magical twists and changes to our set dressing to create the wizarding world.'

Where New York appeared divided into different Muggle and magical locations, Paris leads more of a double life. Whenever a character makes the transition into the wizarding variation on the street, the same streets had to be redressed accordingly.

A DOUBLE WORLD

There is a Paris *within* Paris that can only be entered into by wizards (or in the company of wizards). As with New York and London, this meant taking real elements and flavours of the city and giving them a magical spin, as focused around the shopping district of Place Cachée.

This is one of the things Eddie Redmayne finds so intoxicating about J.K. Rowling's world. 'We all live in cities, but the idea that you can peel something back and find a more vibrant magical world beneath is such an escapist idea.

Above: Using a fluffy cat toy, Newt attempts to lure the Zouwu from the streets of Paris and into his case. *Opposite:* Set extension design by Christian Huband of a street scene that would form the background to most of the Circus Arcanus scenes. *Inset:* Graphic designs for brasserie tiles.

Paris is the perfect tapestry for Jo to start gently unfolding this other world full of whimsy and extraordinary things.'

The question for the designers and indeed students of magical logic was less how to portray a magical Paris but *where* exactly was this magical Paris? Ostensibly, the very same shops, cafes and bars have both a magical and a non-magical version, requiring a significant change to the dressing.

For the magical complexion of the city they created a cauldron shop as if it were a cookery store with different types of copper cooking equipment. 'But in a very magical way,' says prop modeller Pierre Bohanna, 'with some really mad jelly moulds in fish and dragon shapes.'

They were looking not only at a wizarding magical variation on the period, but a wizarding variation of what was *French*. 'The French have such a slightly different way of thinking about things,' says Bohanna. 'So we were thinking about things such as what French Quidditch equipment would be like.'

There are some beautiful Art Nouveau broomsticks hanging in the window of a Quidditch store. And mad, oblique equipment among the wizarding supplies: crystals, telescopes and scientific contraptions. 'All sorts of weird, wacky stuff,' says Bohanna.

The wand shop is very grand, with a window display in the style of a Cartier jeweller.

'We had one person just doing signage for the whole film,' says Mina. 'That includes fascias, hanging signs, awnings, advertisements, and sometimes painted glass for every shop. And twice because of it changing from Muggle to magical.'

This is a citywide extension of the ideology behind platform nine-and-three-quarters at King's Cross Station — a magical version of the same place existing in parallel but invisible to non-wizards. The same is true of MACUSA occupying an alternative dimension of the Woolworth Building.

The portal is found in Montmartre, near the Sacré Coeur, where there is a statue of a woman on a stone plinth. You simply walk through the plinth and pass into magical Paris.

'The two sides feel like they coexist,' says Heyman, 'it feels organic.'

TiNA GOLDSTEIN

toughens up

Magically speaking, things are looking up for Tina. In the months since Newt Scamander departed New York, she has been reinstated as an Auror — the wizarding community's law enforcement — and rediscovered her talent for both magic and investigation. At MACUSA, Tina now counts as a pretty powerful witch.

'She's got her old job back, and in the middle of a mission,' says Katherine Waterston. 'Back in the thick of it, and she's thriving in that position. What she learned in the first film was that although she was nervous about what was going to happen with her career, she never fully lost her confidence in following her instincts, which led them to Grindelwald's arrest. Her core confidence was always there. It was just a little shaken.'

Ever the canny detective, Tina's leads have brought her to Paris, on what Waterston classifies as a 'pro bono' mission. She is still determined to find Credence, the abused orphan who harbours a deadly Obscurus. 'It's a little unclear whether MACUSA knows her whereabouts,' says Waterston. 'Tina isn't confident they would approve of her desire to save Credence. They are seeking him for a different reason.'

Tina's empathy for the young man lies at the heart of the character. The fact that she and Queenie were orphaned very young and Tina felt a responsibility to protect and take care of Queenie, has expanded beyond her sister. 'A child in need, that's her Achilles heel,' says Waterston. 'She'll break the rules to help protect any child. That is what initially drew her to Credence. At the end of the first film, she gave him her word that she and Newt would protect him and she's not one to go back on her word.'

In the two years between *Fantastic Beasts* films, Waterston has hardly paused for breath. She confronted terror among the stars in *Alien: Covenant* and crime shenanigans in *Logan Lucky*, as well as completing three indie dramas. Buoyed by the response to the first film, she was confident she really understood what was going on beneath Tina's cool veneer, particularly her connection to Newt.

Romantically speaking, things couldn't have got worse for Tina. She and Newt had been separated by the Atlantic Ocean but had at least been writing. This was ended abruptly when Tina discovered that Newt is engaged to Leta Lestrange (the witch whose photo he kept in his shed). This is all a ridiculous misunderstanding, of course, but interpersonal communication was never either of their strong suits.

'She has to move on with her life,' explains Waterston. 'She has her work to do, which is Tina's way of coping with painful things. So off to Paris she goes. But then Newt shows up and risks messing up her investigation as he chases her around insisting she listen to his version of what happened.'

In the end, the long-awaited reunion of the

oddball couple may not be quite as romantic as fans had envisaged. 'There's every chance that she might kick him in the shins,' says Waterston. 'She's mad and thinks she's been jilted. She's got her pride. She's trying to cover up how hurt she is, but of course he [Newt] can see through that.'

This stuttering relationship is another wonderful example of what is so real and human about J.K. Rowling's writing. Matters of the heart are beyond the reach of spells. And as the various perils mount up on and below the streets of Paris, Tina finds she is once again having a ball in Newt's company. 'It's like, "Oh, god, this guy's fun to be around", and she has to deal with the fact that he's wonderful and she can't have him.'

To add to Tina's woes, there has been this whole drama with Queenie. Put it this way, the stubborn Goldstein sisters do not see eye to eye on Queenie's somewhat intense marital plans concerning Jacob.

'That was a big responsibility for Alison and I,' says Waterston, 'to bring this history, that you don't see play out, to the film. The fracturing of their relationship is an extraordinary loss for Tina. The film as a whole really explores important lessons about dealing with and confronting the troubled relationships in your life. In a way, while Tina's desperately trying to save Credence, she misses some opportunities to repair

her relationship with Queenie before it's too late.'

Tina's singlemindedness can be seen in her new look. She wears a long, leather coat like those worn by the classic movie detectives. It lends her an aura of power. You wouldn't mess with this lady in a hurry. But it is also like a suit of armour, protecting a fragile heart.

She is sporting a more stylish haircut too, curling across her cheeks.

'In the first film, her hair was so blunt and simple,' says Waterston. 'For the new film, I had been thinking how the romance with Newt had awakened that part of her life. There is now an awareness of herself as someone who could be attractive. I thought that for the first time in her life she would actually go to the hairdressers.'

COLLEEN ATWOOD ON TINA

Tina is now strictly business. 'She's a more powerful woman,' says Atwood. They had tried a dress along the lines of MACU-SA's Seraphina Picquery, but Waterston felt strongly they should stick with trousers. 'Even though Tina has grown more confident that doesn't mean she has become a different person,' says Atwood. 'And when the coat happened, it was such a great coat with pants she ended up back in trousers.'

The overcoat is impressive but heavy. 'It was a workout just to put it on every day,' says Waterston, but admits it helps define her character. 'She has more authority now.'

Atwood is satisfied with the outcome. 'With that amazing blue leather coat, with its cinch waist, she looks like a true detective.'

Left to right: Tina and Newt enter Grindelwald's rally; Tina's reappointment makes the front pages; Newt holds Tina's newspaper cover; Tina is imprisoned in Kama's lair; *Spellbound* magazine causes an unfortunate misunderstanding. *Inset:* A new costume for her new role as an Auror.

FAE HAMMOND · HAIR & MAKE-UP

Returning to the Fantastic Beasts saga, Fae Hammond now feels she is on a journey with these characters. 'This is like stage two,' says the hair and make-up designer, 'with our old faithful cast and a lot of new faces. We've come to Europe, and we've looked very carefully at that European influence on everything, and the effect it has on our characters. There is definitely a different feel to this one.'

For nearly four decades, Hammond has been in the business of making actors look good (or bad if required). The backbone of her career has been in British film, enterprises as diverse as *Layer Cake*, *Nil By Mouth*, and *Pride and Prejudice*. But she

has enjoyed the progression into bigger worlds.

'It's great to have my team back,' she says, 'with all of the same artists doing the same people again. Everybody knew each other, which is a massive thing. You just carry on where you left off.'

On a busy day with up to 500 extras on set, they have three make-up trailers, says Hammond, 'full to the gunwales.' Typically, though, it will be her inner circle of eight trusted collaborators (for the principal actors), with an extra 'truck for prosthetics' whenever Brontis Jodorowsky was due to be transformed into 600-year-old Nicolas Flamel ('A slightly ghostly character'). Hammond is personally responsible for turning Dan Fogler into a slightly more dapper Jacob Kowalski.

Make-up artists work long shifts. Up with the larks to have the actors ready for set, and there at the end of the day to return them to reality. Which can involve encouragement as much as foundation. 'You have to be sensitive,' says Hammond. 'You need to work around any nerves.' They are often the last face an actor sees before they begin a scene. Tact is as important as a brush.

Now that they have fixed their bearings in this earlier era of the wizarding world, there has been a willingness to take chances. 'We have got a lot of artistic licence,' explains Hammond. 'For example, with Leta Lestrange's hair we found pictures of exactly the haircut we wanted to do. But we're just pushing the style. It's a very important balance. Leta's strong finger-waves are great on Zoë [Kravitz], but we add a bit more style.'

Within the screenplay, J.K. Rowling isn't particularly strict in her descriptions — something else which grants Hammond a degree of freedom. 'Casting gives you a direction, but it is really this lovely open book to work with.'

Overall, for the second film, the hair colours are strong. 'The colour spectrum is lovely,' she says. 'We have really black blacks on Grindelwald's acolytes, and blonde blondes and red reds. We've looked at colours from the period. Hair dye was invented not long before this date, and everyone was experimenting. We've taken that a little further — to see how brave we can be without distracting.'

Generally, the era emphasized short hair on a man, but they've left it much longer at the front. 'Or maybe it's a little asymmetric,' she notes. 'You spend hours looking at photographs. There are some extraordinary images: women with men's haircuts, and those big crispy waves that were coming in.'

In fact, Hammond plays an essential part in creating characters. A process that begins with a discussion with the director, before she puts together her famous mood boards and goes to see what Colleen Atwood is thinking in terms of costume.

'Then we come down to three looks,' she explains. 'It is about how far we can push things, but there's always a fine line. Finding that line is what is so enjoyable.'

One thing she has noticed is that Yates has done a lot more close-ups this time. 'We can't get away with anything — the camera is everywhere, like these incredible circular shots around Zoë.'

Opposite: Fae Hammond supervises the make-up for Nicolas Flamel (Brontis Jodorowsky) on set. *Right:* Eddie Redmayne's wig is carefully finished prior to filming. *Far right:* Even minor characters, such as Melusine (Olwen Fouéré), who are on screen for moments, receive just as much attention to ensure everything is perfect.

At the mention of Leta Lestrange, talk turns to the sequel's looks for the main characters and new arrivals...

Newt: 'Eddie Redmayne was very keen to stick with the hair. He loved its sort of oddness, without it being distracting. With everybody else in the movie their hair goes back, Eddie's goes forward. Eddie has the same toupee, with same light colour. It goes well with the little tan that we put on him. His silhouette has become pretty iconic. Even in a dark alley you know it is him. Which is key because we do shoot quite dark sometimes.'

Theseus: 'Callum Turner has good hair, but we had to lighten it to match Eddie's. The biggest thing with Theseus is that Callum has not got a freckle on his face. One of my team, Emmy Beech, took about fifty minutes to carefully freckle him up. It's a work of art. I think the boys look great together. They look like brothers.'

Tina: 'She is back to being an Auror again so we felt that she had to be more chic this time, but still with that simple but gorgeous bob. We *umm*ed and *ahh*ed about the fringe, but David decided he really liked it. That's the big difference. On the first film, it was like maybe Queenie had cut it. Now, you know, she's been to a new salon.'

Queenie: 'Queenie is on a journey. She is not in her comfort zone anymore. We see her soaked in the rain in literally the third scene, and we carry on throughout the movie with her a bit bedraggled. She isn't all glossy curls anymore. She's searching. She's on the run. She is still very pretty, but that polished sort of bubbly look has gone.'

Credence: 'We have moved on from the bowl cut! What's exciting is that we see him leaving New York with a hat, beneath which we spot a shaved head. The idea is that when he eventually arrives in Paris he fits in with the crowd. He's got a simple crop — a grown-out version of the shaved head. Quite dark. We've kept him quite tired looking, quite dirty, almost bestial.'

Kama: 'A fascinating character. There is this underlying, mystical elegance. He's got naturally very curly hair, which he wears in a calm, elegant wave.'

Dumbledore and Hogwarts: 'This was very exciting. It's quite phenomenal to go there. Seeing a young Newt and a young Leta. It's a case of following the iconography, but putting that bit of period in there. Jude Law was great. David wanted Dumbledore to be very natural, with a beard, but nothing huge. Just someone you really believe is a professor, as if he was from Oxford. I looked at painters and artists to try and get that lovely lived-in feeling of someone who doesn't really come out of the schoolroom.'

YUSUF KAMA

Elegantly suited, if a little frayed at the edges, with a black vulture feather sticking out from his jaunty hat, Yusuf Kama is like no one we have met before in the Wizarding World. Of French-African ancestry, he has come to Paris obsessed with keeping a promise — a promise that may involve Credence.

Classically trained actor William Nadylam, who is French-Italian by upbringing, with a Cameroonian father and Indian mother, established himself in Paris theatre before branching into film and television. He brings a natural gift for a theatrical flourish.

'Yusuf Kama is African,' he states . 'He comes from Senegal. In Africa, magic is everywhere. My dad was a doctor, and he was always in competition with the local sorcerer. And he was someone who *knew* things.'

Nadylam has long been drawn to the Harry Potter universe. 'It's a parallel life where we can actually fly, like a dream,' he says. Nonetheless, it is J.K. Rowling's determination not to paint characters as simply good or evil that excited

him. 'I remember the shock I had, a real shock, when I discovered that Dumbledore was not necessarily who I thought he was. You realize he had his own doubts. He was once a friend of Grindelwald. No one is innocent here.'

Lurking in a hideout on the banks of the Seine, Kama has clearly fallen on hard times. 'He is the son of a great, great wizard,' explains Nadylam. 'He was living a happy life in a quite protected environment, an aristocratic upbringing. And all of a sudden it stops, he's lost his mother and father and has had to redefine himself and find his bearings.'

What he has been left with is this hunger for revenge. Before he died, his father bound him to an Unbreakable Vow to avenge his family. If he breaks such a magical bond he will die.

The wizard carries with him a copy of *The Predictions of Tycho Dodonus*, an obscure tome full of extraordinary prophecies. On the wall of his lair are scribbled the complex equations of his family tree.

'Kama touched on a lot of fibres inside me,' says Nadylam. 'I'm really trapped in this character

Top: Kama studies his obsessively drawn investigation into his ancestry. *Above:* Prop of *The Predictions of Tycho Dodonus.* Opposite. Kama's search leads him to the circus.

because it is so close to me. He doesn't exactly know who he is. He's basically in a quest for his identity. The same questions are in there from the first Harry Potter — where do you belong? He needs someone else to help him see the light.'

KAMA'S LAIR

Yusuf Kama has been hiding out in a dismal, subterranean chamber that runs beneath the Seine. It also turns out to be close to the Paris sewer system. It is here he imprisons Tina, Newt and Jacob, bringing about an unexpected reunion. It is here too that he reveals his obsession with Credence.

'It has a very low ceiling,' says Craig, who drew inspiration from the sewer scenes in the classic film noir *The Third Man*. 'The roof of this riverside complex, and the tunnel that leads into it, are in fact under the arch of the bridge that joins with the bank.'

'Stuart based his design on underground waterworks,' explains set decorator Anna Pinnock, 'so our task was to recreate a pumping system from this era from various items we found, with Pierre Bohanna's team adding suitable embellishment.'

It is here Tina is confronted with the sight of Kama's calculations of the Lestrange family tree scribbled over the walls.

'Kama is obsessed with how Credence might connect with the Lestrange family,' says Craig. 'The graphics on the walls of this massive tunnel, and roof above him, reveal he has been obsessively trying to work out a connection with Credence, and then track him down and kill him.'

Still, the atmosphere is dank and unhealthy, and keen-eyed Newt will later spot that Kama has become infected, as a parasite plops into the water.

Once he and Tina escape, it is up on the bridge where Newt will attempt to subdue the escaped Zouwu — using a fluffy toy on a stick.

COLLEEN ATWOOD ON YUSUF KAMA

'He is an unusual character whose African origins are quite different from anything we've seen before,' says Atwood of the new arrival. 'Like Leta, he is an aristocrat in his world, but has fallen on hard times: his clothes are worn-out. He hasn't had anything new for a long time. But what he has is of the highest quality.'

The actor, William Nadylam, has what Atwood considered a 'classical, theatrical bearing.' This prompted a distinctive hat, with a feather sprouting from the band, to pull it all together.

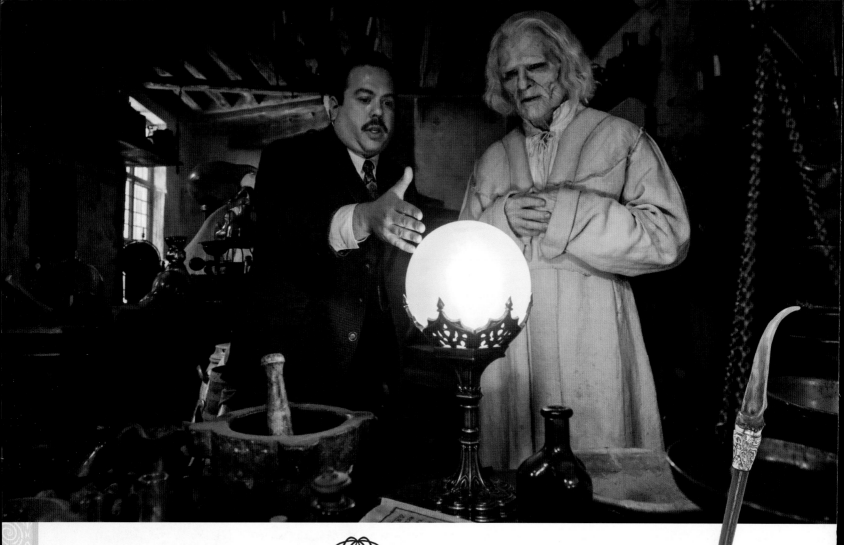

NICOLAS FLAMEL

The eccentric Nicolas Flamel is based upon a real person — who may or may not have been immortal. The genuine Flamel was a fourteenth-century scribe who lived and worked in Paris. Ironically, following his death, rumours abounded that he was a mythical alchemist who had discovered the Philosopher's Stone that turned lead into gold and provided him with everlasting life.

This arcane figure, of course, had a big influence on J.K. Rowling's very first Harry Potter novel, where we encounter his fabled artefact, if not its keeper. The author has finally introduced Flamel in person, equipped with immortality — the script places him at a sprightly 600 years of age — and resident at 51 Rue de Montmorency, a house that still stands in Paris. Although the architecture and content have been transformed for the purposes of fiction.

'It's a restaurant now, I think,' says Brontis Jodorowsky, the French-Mexican actor playing the antiquated wizard. 'When J.K. Rowling visited the place they showed her the written formula of the Philosopher's Stone.'

Crucially, when it comes to the second *Fantastic Beasts* film, Flamel is an ally of Dumbledore, and his tumbledown house, stocked with the dusty paraphernalia of his alchemical pursuits, offers a haven for Newt, Jacob and Tina.

As well as his acting talents, Jodorowsky doubly fits the bill, given his father is Chilean cult director Alejandro Jodorowsky, director of the mystical Western *El Topo* and *Holy Mountain*, which follows a powerful alchemist's quest for enlightenment. That said, his son has leant as much on his mother's French side to portray Flamel, as well as his birthplace of Mexico. 'In

Top: Jacob sees a vision in Flamel's crystal ball; the white glow will be replaced with visual effects in the finished film. *Inset:* Flamel's wand features a dragon's claw.

Mexico, magic exists,' he says.

He admits it was impossible to conceive of what it would be like to be a 600-year-old man. Would he even be able to walk? It was easier to think of him as having been magically preserved at ninety-something. Which still required the daily application of layers of mottled prosthetics to the fifty-five-year-old actor.

'It is very interesting for me because I don't look like this in real life at all,' he says. 'And I don't consider myself an old person. It's a process where you have to erase yourself and become someone else. The prosthetics are another costume. You could say, it's a very alchemical process.'

Costume designer Colleen Atwood not only played upon his great age, but the fact this is a wizard who is also a scientist of his time. 'I had to think about what he would wear when he was working, in tandem with his pale hair and skin,' she says, and came up with a medieval version of a lab coat. Like Newt, Flamel is another example of Rowling's thematic marriage of science and magic.

Flamel's wand, says Jodorowsky, is a very beautiful object. 'It has a dragon claw,' he says proudly. 'But a wand, you'll remember, is an extension of your soul. The wand chooses the sorcerer, and this one has chosen me.'

A MAGICAL BOOK

When owls are not secure enough, the hip wizard turns to a magical book to get in touch with their magical friends.

'A bit like the Marauder's Map, it's a clever device Jo has come up with to make things happen,' explains Miraphora Mina, whose team has been responsible for creating it. 'It looks like a book but each page is a picture of someone in their office.'

'Like a photo album,' adds her partner Eduardo Lima.

'You can talk to wizards in your circle, a sort of WhatsApp group,' laughs Mina. Much like the moving portraits on the walls of Hogwarts, each page in this magical directory will show that witch or wizard. If they're not in, you just see their office.

They had been meeting with Rowling and director David Yates about something else entirely, when the author mentioned this clever new concept she had in mind for Dumbledore to get in touch with Flamel. 'And we had ten days to come up with the book,' says Lima. 'Working in the wizarding world keeps you on your toes.'

For the design, they looked at old Victorian photo albums with a very heavy card for the pages, which gave them the stability to contain a window into another world. They also followed antique bookbinding techniques to give the outside an appropriately old-world style. On the cover is an ornate phoenix in gold tooled into the leather.

THE ANCIENT ABODE OF NICOLAS FLAMEL

History tells us that Nicolas Flamel genuinely lived on the Rue de Montmorency in fourteenth-century Paris. In fact, he is still residing there in the early part of the twentieth century and the second *Fantastic Beasts* adventure: wizard, apothecary and alchemist, and inventor of the fabled Philosopher's Stone, which has bestowed such longevity upon him.

'He is six hundred years old,' explains production designer Stuart Craig. 'So we've given him a timber-framed house. In England the closest thing would be the Tudor style; in Paris it is a fifteenth-century oak-framed dwelling.'

It is certainly distinctive, leaning at an alarming angle, with an antiquity to match its tenant. That sense of oddness and age continues within the crammed apothecary, a smoky interior teeming with cauldrons, retorts, vials, potions, and dusty alchemical bric-a-brac, with shelves crammed with faded leather volumes.

'It was a big set dressing job for Anna Pinnock, that she enjoyed very much,' says Craig. The set decorator had a ball raiding the flea markets of the French capital for every specimen of antique scientific paraphernalia she could lay her hands on — the more decrepit the better.

'It was such a wonderfully layered and aged set, with so many unexpected nooks and crannies filled with dusty spell books and unusual things,' she says. 'Much of it was from the French Middle Ages as Flamel is so old. But it is equally full of more modern, Victorian chemistry alongside the ancient alchemical contraptions.'

The challenge was to combine the mysteriousness of Flamel's background with the sense of a haven for the heroes who have a series of long scenes in his back room. Newt and Tina have come here in search of help, with Flamel a long associate of Dumbledore's. The Hogwarts professor had passed along Flamel's business card to the Magizoologist.

Thus the graphic design team had to consider what a 600-year-old wizard's business card might look like.

'Would he have a business card from the twenties?' asks graphic designer Eduardo Lima rhetorically. 'Or would he have something that suggests it's much older, before even business cards existed? We made this little, wooden card, very thin like veneer.'

Flamel's symbol, which we also see outside his workshop, magically sears its way onto the blank card. 'It's the symbol first,' he notes, 'and then the name appears.'

For the colourful actor Brontis Jodorowsky, who fills the Methuselah-like stockings of the wizened wizard, being enveloped by such detail fired his imagination. 'An actor's main tool is his imagination,' he says. 'It's absolutely fantastic to have sets like this to work with. The scenes are so powerful and so full of images, you only need to blend in and believe.'

Of great significance to fans, of course, will be the presence of the Philosopher's Stone, as seen in the very first Harry Potter film and now idly resting on a stand within a glass bell jar. Anyone who has taken the Warner Bros. Studio Tour at Leavesden will know that the original, red-quartz stone still exists (in fact, there are several).

'We had to make new ones,' explains Bohanna, 'because the ones we made on *Philosopher's Stone*, in a prop-making sense, had lost a lot of their lustre. They'd been handled a lot, so we had to remould it and freshen it up.'

Even immortal stones don't last forever.

Opposite: Concept art of the immortal alchemist's house by Peter Popken. *Inset:* Prop of Flamel's business card given by Dumbledore to Newt. *Left:* A meticulously dressed set full of props reveals the alchemist's tools of his trade. *Below:* The fabulous Philosopher's Stone is kept under a glass bell jar.

LE MINISTÈRE DES AFFAIRES MAGIQUES DE LA FRANCE

MINISTRIES OF THE WORLD

We were introduced to the British Ministry of Magic in the Harry Potter films, an ornate, layer-cake of Whitehall offices deep underground, and accessed via a red telephone box. Then in the first *Fantastic Beasts* film, the towering MACUSA was found hidden inside the Woolworth Building in New York. And now in Paris we will discover the French variation on the theme — the grandly titled Le Ministère des Affaires Magiques de la France. Which, naturally, boasts its idiosyncratic twist on institutional architecture.

In fact, the sequel will be the first film in the Wizarding World to feature three different ministries. Before the film heads to Paris, it will stop by MACUSA's rooftop and the Ministry of Magic in Whitehall. Where it is the identical building, only seventy years earlier.

'We've used some of the same details as we did in the original Harry Potter version,' confirms Craig. 'All the wall surfaces have this glossy, ceramic tile, which was something we had learned from the London Underground.'

Ceramic is impervious to water, so is the ideal material for damp, subterranean places. In the overbearing Hearing Room, Newt will be pressed by Torquil Travers, Head of Magical Law Enforcement, alongside his brother Theseus, Head of the Auror Office, while an unmanned quill hovers to take notes. From this vantage point we get a new

Newt and Tina enter the Records Room.

angle on the Ministry's subterranean heights. The towering cylinders of offices like stacks of coins encircling a vast atrium.

Using one of a fleet of new-fangled digital design tools, concept artist Dermot Power created a virtual reality mock-up of the set and was delighted to witness a visiting J.K. Rowling in goggles gazing around the fruits of her imagination.

In one of those eccentric touches that give her wizarding world such personality, roving the circular corridor outside the Hearing Room is a lonely, self-propelled vacuum cleaner. The grumpy appliance wheezing its way across the carpet is another speciality of prop modeller Pierre Bohanna.

'For a hoover it's big,' he says. 'It's running around on three wheels, with a massive, ballooning bag on the back.' During the design process, they imagined that the straining hoover bag is in dire need of emptying, and all the dust and rubbish is blowing out the back of it. 'It's making as much mess as it's clearing up,' laughs Bohanna.

The three ministries might differ structurally, but they are all stifled by that wizardly predilection for soul-sapping bureaucracy. It is another of J.K. Rowling's recurring themes: magic or not, all governmental bodies come buried in paperwork.

'The paperwork, all the files and stationery, are very much of the time,' says Miraphora Mina.

'Even the style of the folders is all very twenties.'

For each ministry the graphic design team has a signature colour. For the British establishment it is purple, for MACUSA it's green, and for the Ministère it is blue. You'll see it in the ribbons and folder edges, just a subtle touch of colour to denote a particular brand of magical officialdom.

'If anything, we'll see that France is even more tied up in bureaucracy,' says Mina. 'We have had to create reams of French documentation.'

UNDERNEATH THE DOMES

From J.K. Rowling's explorations of Paris's less frequented corners, the entrance to the Ministère was in part inspired by the picturesque Place de Furstenberg. 'The reasons why are very apparent,' explains Craig. 'Furstenberg is a very modest little square but rather beautiful in its small way. It has four extremely tall, rather elegant trees in each corner, and as you approach there is a little fountain in the middle.'

The roots of those four trees extend into the centre of the square forming a cage over the fountain. The cage turns out to be the Art Nouveau shell of a lift, which then descends to the Ministère, although it isn't, strictly-speaking, underground.

'In the script they get into a lift and go down several floors, like the Ministry of Magic in England, and you get this feeling you are going down deep,' says Power, delighting in another of Stuart Craig's ingenious twists. 'Stuart flipped that and made the French ministry completely lateral.'

The Ministère is made up of a series of beautiful domes like great, glass igloos with interconnecting glass tunnels. A layout that is not dissimilar to the Eden Project in Cornwall.

'So much of the script is at nighttime and underground,' continues Power. 'Even the final scene in the amphitheatre, and Newt's basement is underground. So, though the script seemed to place the Ministère underground, daylight comes through the glass.'

At first, Craig's devoted team had tried to make logical sense of the airy vault. Power had suggested that wizards might go up into the clouds to enter the Ministère. 'Stuart didn't react to that,' he laughs — a sure sign he wasn't keen. 'Because

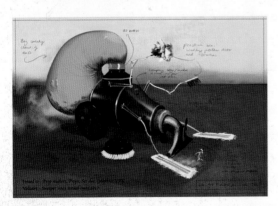

Overleaf: Concept art by Dermot Power reveals the breathtaking Celestial Dome featuring fantastic beasts from around the world; beneath floats an early idea for a magical activity locator, which was later abandoned.

you are not going to have earth on the other side of that glass, you want to draw attention to the glass itself. So what would you do? Would you frost the glass? Stained glass would be too colourful. Then we came up with the idea of a star map.'

Testing the idea, Power pasted pictures from old eighteenth century celestial charts into his 3D rendering of the Ministère, and then set them slowly moving. That way, the ceiling would draw attention to itself, and away from what might be beyond it. 'You distract the viewer from thinking too much by having this beautiful thing to look at.'

Rowling had insisted that, rather than using the real-world zodiac, they create a wizarding world spin on Aries the lamb, Leo the lion, and so on. They would, of course, use fantastic beasts, based on the designs of German artist Albrecht Durer's painstaking sixteenth-century woodcuts.

Power elaborates: 'I created the ceiling using different creatures from the wizarding world; just grabbing them from *Fantastic Beasts* and Harry Potter, and illustrations we had done over the years, and then applied a very quick engraving filter.'

These were temporary placeholders, but Rowling loved it, and started providing notes on which creatures to take out and which to include. 'It's a whole astrology,' he says,

marvelling at how a small idea can expand into a subsection of the mythology.

Mixed in with the moving heavens are details of where the stars lie in each celestial beast, alongside their French names (luckily Power had a French edition of the book): Le Murlap, Le Niffleur, and so forth. There are twenty-five creatures and objects circling the dome, including the Durmstrang ship seen in *Harry Potter and the Goblet of Fire* (Power drew from photographs of the original models) and a water scene with mermaids, Triton and nymphs. He smiles, 'Hopefully it will look weird, and unusual; it has that look of Europe.'

Away from the entrance hall with its dancing ceiling, we will pass into domes for the mailroom, the typing pool, and the ornate Records Room. Everywhere there is the aura of business-like order. Like MACUSA, it is a credibly, functioning government organization.

'This was possibly our only fully Art Nouveau set,' says set decorator Anna Pinnock, and Rowling had been emphatic on the style of the Ministère. 'With the series of domed spaces it was challenging to find a repetitive style of office furniture that could work in rows throughout.'

On one of her shopping trips to Paris, Pinnock discovered an unusual glass and metal desk outside in a flea market. Straightaway, she could see that it could be replicated in great numbers and adapted to work in a modular, linked-up fashion.

'It was cramped to sit at and had a ministerial meanness to its shallow surface,' she says, delighted with the find. 'We also found reproduction French metal chairs on sale in China. We painted them for a more period look.'

For the typing pool — another regular motif — they made over 100 French typewriters and their own interpretation of a tickertape machine. 'Anna herself went to the Science Museum to look at different versions,' explains Bohanna. 'She wanted a certain French feel to it. We came up with the idea that, whereas with the Ministry of Magic, you had paper planes as flying memos, for the Ministère we would do flying tickertape.'

The tickertape literally flies. Ribbons of paper twisting through the air like swimming snakes. On top of each typing pool desk sits a tickertape wheel into which a ribbon of paper would thread before swimming out again on the other side.

RECORDS ROOM

With various parties coming in search of the Lestrange family tree, a major action sequence takes place in the elaborate, tiered arrangement of the Records Room.

'The shelves are rather interesting and beautiful, and Art Nouveau in style,' he says. 'With a sinewy, organic structure to them.' Nonetheless,

Top: Concept art of the Records Room by Dermot Power; the positions of the stacks will move and slide like a puzzle square. *Above*: Tina and Newt are discovered in the Records Room.

by his design, the archive is made up of a series of towering, square, shelving units that move sideways, back and forth, and up and down rather like an old-fashioned tile puzzle.

'Stuart wanted to make it much more mechanical,' says Power. 'That worked well, as the characters were going to be climbing them and hiding in them. Which is a good example of where the design influenced the story.'

Craig continues. 'The search for that Lestrange document is the point of this scene. We have built a series of these tall treelike shelving units, which are topped up by visual effects. Scale is an important feature. In the scale of it lies the theatricality of these rather expressionistic sets.'

At the four corners of the practical set were statues of the same female figure known as Marianne, a symbol of revolutionary France dating back to 1789. 'She is not just associated with the Revolution anymore,' says Craig, 'she is kind of a symbol of France. The entire set has an organic, curving, growing texture. Rather like the trees in the square outside.'

'It was a model-maker's dream,' says Pinnock, 'from the very elaborate and ornate moving shelves that Stuart designed to the equally elaborate and complex archive boxes.'

'That was one of our biggest challenges,' explains Bohanna. 'These file boxes in which the records are contained. We made over 1,200 of these boxes to stock these towers.'

Once the mayhem of the chase is underway, involving a battalion of CGI Matagots, the Ministère's temperamental feline security personnel, the scene switched to a greenscreen set.

'We had to create endless virtual rows of shelves,' says Tim Burke, visual effects supervisor. 'All of those shelves start to animate in this fantastic chase sequence, which we shot with lots of green props for the actors to interact with and dodge. What's great on this film is that the actors are very involved in what we're doing. They're giving us their character beats. So we're getting Eddie Redmayne saying what he would do and Katherine Waterston saying what she would do, and we're developing the story with them. They're giving us ideas for what the creatures would do. It's a real collaboration.'

CIRCUS ARCANUS

Arriving in Paris from New York, Credence is now part of Circus Arcanus. The first circus ever seen within the wizarding world, this surely offers scope for a splendid, magical reworking of a big top extravaganza. However, this particular jamboree doesn't exactly live up to the billing.

'Circus Arcanus is a brutal place,' explains J.K. Rowling. 'It might seem at first glance to be a place of great wonder and mystery, but in fact, it's a combination of freak show and a form of people trafficking.'

'It is very poor and dirty,' remarks costume designer Colleen Atwood. 'In terms of the costumes, there are a lot of chinks in everyone's armour. They are filthy, really brown, and kind of thrown together as opposed to designed.'

There is quite a difference, she points out, between a travelling carny in that old American sense and Rowling's melancholy diversion that has pitched its tents in Place Cachée, in

the vicinity of Montmartre. The set for this neglected circus was built as part of the 3,000 linear foot, Paris backlot complex.

They built three different versions of the main tent: interior, exterior, and damaged, as well as a tiny miniature tent. The visual effects department have added a background where in the moonlit distance can be seen landmarks such as the Sacre Coeur.

The mood, emphasizes Atwood, is poverty. This is more of 'an end of the road' circus. 'If you see a clown,' she says, 'he's more likely a clown whose feet are on backwards. There are a lot of deformities here, halfway between human and creature.'

Like The Blind Pig, the goblin Gnarlak's dingy speakeasy in New York, this shabby establishment reveals the unwholesome lower tiers of the wizarding world. And it is to here Tina that has come in search of Credence.

Circus Arcanus is run by a disreputable wizard by the name of Skender (played by the Icelandic actor Ólafur Darri Ólafsson, who formerly featured as one of the misshapen giants in Steven Spielberg's *The BFG*), who is clearly in it for the money. He stalks this huddle of tents and cages with a staff and wand, terrorising his crew of

Above: The Circus entertains the wizarding community of Paris; *(inset):* graphic art advertising Circus Arcanus attractions, including the Kappa, Oni and the Maledictus.

ONI 鬼 ONI

destitute Underbeings, the sorry descendants of magical beings.

'He's a combination of animal trainer and a ringmaster,' says Atwood, 'so he's got a dark edge to him. He's more complex than a normal ringmaster. He's from a dark place.'

David Yates describes him bluntly as a 'people trafficker.'

Highlighting the theme that runs throughout the Fantastic Beasts films, set decorator Anna Pinnock sees Skender's set-up simply for what it us — a freakshow exploiting these tragic creatures. 'It is a disturbing place,' she iterates. Nevertheless, this squalid circus has presented some interesting challenges for the designers.

The graphics team created a series of period posters using old-time methods, featuring the alluring mystery of the Maledictus. 'The kind of paper we used was not like a traditional paper, the colour was different,' says Eduardo Lima. 'They are also screen printed, which allows a different finish.'

'We designed three big banners for outside the circus,' says fellow graphic designer Miraphora Mina. They always have to take into account who would be designing them *within* the world of the story.

'In this case it would have been Skender's workers,' she says. 'The posters are a little bit more sophisticated — Skender may have looked up a cheap, Paris printer for those and we found some really cool period show fonts.'

Outside the main tent is a muddle of sideshows, street carts, stalls and rusty cages, including an elaborate crate covered in Chinese symbols that houses the Zouwu.

'We really did try and add some subtlety of that period, not make it too layered and modern,' says Stuart Craig. 'It has an old-fashioned feel with lights strung about, which will be extended by visual effects.'

Here at least they got to have a little fun with magical variants on traditional carnies.

Top to bottom: Ólafur Darri Ólafsson is prepared for Skender's scene inside the circus tent; graphic art of a poster advertising the Oni; Skender's wand.

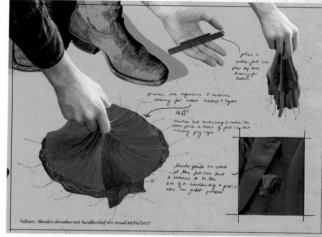

The design team came up with a coconut stall where the coconuts have faces… 'They look like the classic, big-moustachioed, Victorian version of French men,' says special prop designer Pierre Bohanna with a gleeful chuckle.

Extending the theme of the moody vacuum cleaner at the Ministry in London, Bohanna created an accordion with a mind of its own. 'Basically, the accordion player is sitting down playing the accordion and the accordion bellows turn into arms and legs and it starts dancing to its own music.'

Inside the sweaty, overcrowded interior of the main tent is a large cage in which the creatures and misfits are paraded. Far from a classic big top soaring with trapeze artists, it is simply a chance for the wizarding public to stand and gawp at the sad aberrations.

'There was ample and interesting research for circuses of the time: reference pictures,' says Craig, noting that this kind of bargain-basement travelling museum had been quite common in Europe in Victorian times.

With an ingenious touch of Rowling magic, when they are due to head off to the next town, Skender simply shrinks the main tent down to the size of a handkerchief and stows it in his pocket.

Circus Arcanus also features a menagerie of fantastic but rather depressed creatures brought to life using digital effects.

Caged, chained or housed in tanks according to their natures, Skender's collection contains an enraged Zouwu, a Kappa, and an Oni. And, of course, the Maledictus, swapping skin for snake scale. In the corner of the main tent, stands a reinforced cage filled with irritable Firedrakes sending out the occasional shower of sparks.

Top to bottom: One of the cast's extras receives instructions prior to filming a crowd scene; production design showing how the circus tent will shrink to the size of a handkerchief that fits in Skender's pocket; concept art by Paul Catling shows the Kappa and the Oni sharing a cramped cage; Skender and an eager audience wait to see what the Maledictus will do next. *Overleaf:* The Circus Arcanus exterior sits in the junction of the enormous and fully dressed Paris street set.

THE
UNDERBEINGS

BEHIND THE SCENES AT THE CIRCUS ARCANUS,

pitiful Underbeings shuffle around taking money from the crowd, feeding the creatures and cleaning up at the end of night. The odd one might perform, but they are a browbeaten bunch. Underbeings, you see, form a lower caste of the wizarding world: a subset of misshapen, mixed-up humanoids that have magical ancestry but, unlike the house-elves from the Harry Potter films, possess no actual powers.

'They are kind of in-between human and creature, I guess,' muses costume designer Colleen Atwood, 'and they have made the idea of being an entertainer work. It allows them to put on this thin skin of recognizability to be in the human world and not be in cages like the creatures at the circus.'

This new classification to the wizarding world typically encompasses half-elves, half-goblins, and half-trolls. A half-troll can be seen performing feats of strength, while half-elves and half-goblins juggle and tumble. But mostly this crew of outsiders take pains to conceal their true natures as well as they can. Horns are hidden beneath hats, protruding eyes beneath hoods.

On film, rather than fully computer-generated like the full-blown elves, something more poignant is achieved by casting real people and then adding a layer of digital augmentation. The actors' faces are scanned, turned into a texture map, and then exaggerated by the visual effects wizards.

Opposite: One of the circus Underbeings towers above a crew member as they carry out final checks on his costume.

CREDENCE'S
journey of self-discovery

Credence is no longer Credence Barebone. Following the death of his adoptive mother at his own, uncontrolled hand, and his arrival in Paris, he is known only as Credence. Once again, this troubled young man is unwittingly the eye of the storm. No less than five separate parties are in pursuit of him, each with their own agenda for the tragic Obscurial: Tina is desperate to save him, Newt as well, but Yusuf Kama, Grimmson and, worst of all, Grindelwald have something less savoury in mind.

'Well, you could with justice, have believed that Credence had been killed at the end of the first film,' says J.K. Rowling. 'But, in fact, as Newt knows, you can't kill an Obscurial when they're in their Obscurus form. You can shatter the Obscurus temporarily, but the person hasn't died. So Credence survives and his big question now is, "Who am I?" And so his quest for his true identity propels his story through the second movie. One of the major strands in this movie, is, who is Credence?'

Ezra Miller admits that he had an inkling of what Credence might face in the new film, as Rowling had supplied him with 'little indications' of what was next for the runaway Obscurial.

'She told me about the circus and that there would be a Maledictus there, and she told me the essence of Credence's arc — that he was on a journey looking for his birth mother.'

Miller's performance as the troubled adoptee harbouring a terrible magical force was one of the highlights of the first film. The highly talented actor managing to portray Credence's plight as both unnervingly eerie and very moving, both a lost boy and potential apocalypse.

'Credence is a young man with a severely troubled and traumatic history,' explains Miller, who is a proud Harry Potter super-fan. 'Through an act of only partially intentional violence, having cast off the chains of his abuse, he is now setting out on a journey of self-discovery, because much of what he knew of himself he knows now to be a lie.'

Before being adopted by the tyrannical Mary Lou Barebone in New York, Credence had been born to an unnamed witch. Now he is driven by the possibility of discovering the identity of his mother — who may have a connection to the Lestrange family tree — and thereby find his place in the world. He also hopes that by understanding where he came from he will gain mastery over the Obscurus within him — that vortex of parasitic magic manifested as an inky, roiling cloud.

'He is already starting to gain a measure of control, to manifest the Obscurus intentionally,' says Miller, who between films swapped magic for superheroics as the hyperactive Flash in *Justice League*. 'There's a liberation and relief to that. He is transforming into someone who is surviving. Which brings with

it burdens of choice and responsibility, but he's still a kind of unexploded bomb because of his inherent power.'

The fact that he is even alive is a miracle. Credence has reached the point in a wizard's life when the Obscurus would normally have killed them. As Miller sees it, survival has become a mechanism of discovery. 'He knows his mother who gave him up is in Europe. He has an adoption paper.'

The tragic irony is that Grindelwald has the knowledge of Credence's true identity.

'It's a very tragic chapter,' says Miller. 'One that speaks to the archetypal journey that Credence is on.'

Credence is now part of a wizarding circus run by the disreputable Skender. Populated with outcasts from the magical world — and some seriously neglected beasts — this soon proves to be another abusive environment.

Above: Credence and the Maledictus enjoy a quiet moment together; *(inset)* Atwood created a whole new costume for the character in Paris: *Opposite (top to bottom):* Credence and the Maledictus head towards a dramatic rendezvous; Credence's adoption certificate; Credence learns more about his ancestry; Standing in the Lestrange mausoleum, Credence and the Maledictus witness a revelation.

In this forlorn freakshow, Credence will form an attachment to a young woman with her own magical malady. This beautiful girl, played by Claudia Kim, is a Maledictus — afflicted with a blood curse, she is slowly but irrevocably transforming into a snake.

'There is a real love there between these two people,' says Miller, 'carrying these otherworldly aspects of themselves that have removed them from society. But it is also a codependency; two people who are trapped in hourglasses with the sand trickling away.'

The tragic fate of the
MALEDICTUS

Among the many, sorry sideshows at Circus Arcanus is to be found a Maledictus. According to the arcane details of J.K. Rowling's wizarding lore, a Maledictus is a human afflicted with a blood curse, which sees them gradually transform in to a beast (the name derives from the word 'malediction' meaning curse). What is true is that the curse is irrevocable — at some point in time they will lose their human side entirely.

The Maledictus in question is cursed to become a snake, while her human form is played by South Korean actress Claudia Kim.

Kim takes up the story. 'The circus is this dark, terrible place where these misfits of magical beings have been captured by this abusive man named Skender. The Maledictus is a prisoner in this place. She is also bound to become a prisoner in her own body. But it is in this place of hopelessness she meets Credence.'

Two outsiders, each a victim of magical forces inside of them, they are naturally drawn to one another.

'She embodies this incredible power,' says Kim, 'but every day she feels the curse taking over her. The clock is ticking, and all she wants to do is stay a woman for as long as she can and find love in Credence.'

Her serpentine double nature can be seen in her startling, skin-tight dress. For Kim it was more than a costume, it was a vivid extension of the character. 'That dress fit me like a glove. I was just wowed by it, from the early sketches to the final product. The Maledictus lives in it every single day — it's like her own skin, and she suffers in it. They captured the beauty and tragedy of her in that dress.'

As Kim says, there is a sad beauty to her choices. The Maledictus is able to set aside her own desires to help Credence pursue his quest and heal himself. Even though she knows her doom is inevitable, that one day she will be forever trapped in the body of a snake, escaping from the circus has given her a freedom she has never dreamt of having.

'There's a wonderful partnership between them,' says Kim. 'Credence brings out the woman in her. She becomes nurturing and protective to him.'

When at first Credence's attempts to locate his mother are thwarted, he seizes onto the hope that Grindelwald knows the truth about him. It's a highly risky measure that threatens to split these lonely souls apart. When it comes to Grindelwald, adds Kim, 'the Maledictus knows by instinct that he's up to no good.'

COLLEEN ATWOOD ON THE MALEDICTUS

When dressing actress Claudia Kim, the challenge was to encompass her character's gradual transformation into a snake. 'I saw her as like the Apache dancers that they had in Paris in the twenties,' says Atwood. Pronounced 'ah-*Pash*', and slang for the savage gangs of the Parisian underworld, this street dance was a theatrical form of combat that made its way eventually to the Moulin Rouge.

'It had this destructive Tango vibe to it,' explains Atwood, 'and I was basing her dress on those dancers. I found lace that had a pattern that was similar to snakeskin. It's this midnight blue colour, with foil glaze over the lace to kick it up a little bit more.'

Given actual serpentine transfigurations would be the province of the visual effects department, Atwood consulted with the digital artists beforehand. 'I showed them the fabric and the design, talked to them, and they were really happy with it.'

This kind of synergy is crucial. Across all her costumes Atwood has to constantly keep in mind how her design will work in regards to any visual or practical effects, or indeed stuntwork. 'For the Maledictus' dress, we had a contortionist come in and do some work in the real thing, to see how it looked when stretched out and distorted.'

There hangs over this extraordinary character an uncertain future, which even Kim has no knowledge of yet. 'I trust J.K. Rowling and David completely. She just gives us these little hints. And we're like, "Give us more! Give us more!" But so far she wants to leave my future as a mystery.'

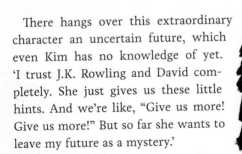

Top: The Maledictus laments her uncertain fate. *Middle:* A Dark moment for the Maledictus. *Left:* Graphic art of a Circus Arcanus poster. *Right:* the Maledictus wearing her beautiful blue snakeskin dress. *Far right:* Framed prints of the attractions adorn the Circus Arcanus tent set.

ANNA PINNOCK · SET DECORATION

Put simply, the art of set decoration is the sourcing and positioning of all those elements in a scene that count as neither set or actor. If it's not tied down then it's the proverbial set decoration. 'I arrange everything inside the walls,' says the head of the department, Anna Pinnock, stressing that it is a very close collaboration across the whole production with prop makers, costume designers, model makers, graphic designers, and sculptors.

Most of what Pinnock provides falls under the banner of props. Which in the case of the wizarding world can range from antique light fittings to shop awnings to broomsticks.

Pinnock is a six-time Academy Award nominee, including a nomination for *Fantastic Beasts and Where to Find Them*, and a win for *The Grand Budapest Hotel*. She has worked on three James Bond movies, and, prior to her return to the Wizarding World, with Steven Spielberg on virtual reality adventure *Ready Player One*. So she knows her way around a set.

She suggests that there are certain advantages to this being the second film in a

A fantastic variety of pots, bowls and containers was sourced by Pinnock's team in order to populate this intricately dressed cauldron shop set.

franchise. The world has been established. They are also now charting a course closer to the aesthetic set down by a hugely successful sister set of films in the same universe.

On the first *Fantastic Beasts*, she had deliberately avoided getting too immersed in the Harry Potter films, determined to bring a fresh approach to Newt's adventures. The sequel, however, she recognizes, has 'connections and nuances' with the older films. 'In this film, I've made a conscious effort to pay homage to the Harry Potter fans a bit more, and be more attentive to the world I've entered. I feel very much more part of this world.'

For all the familiarity, the new film is a departure. 'It has very intricate thriller-like whodunit plot,' she observes. 'The characters develop, deepen and change.' All of which effects what she does, as in her hands every set is an extension of both plot and character.

The thrill of working with J.K. Rowling is that her imagination seems inexhaustible. The script boasted brand new locations to decorate in New York, London, and most prominently Paris. If they are returning to recognizable haunts, they are viewed from enticing new angles. We will see a Hogwarts long before Harry Potter arrived, where Dumbledore's Defence Against the Dark

Arts class is outfitted to reflect his fascinations: the polished paraphernalia of astronomy, being one; the challenge of a Boggart-inhabited wardrobe being another.

What really inspires Pinnock is that, while it is a complete fantasy world, realized to an extraordinary degree by Rowling, it is simultaneously a real-world twenties backdrop. She and her team must have looked through thousands of photographs from the era. Research has also been crucial in order to 'knowingly depart' from period accuracy.

Ultimately, Paris has widened the palette, especially with the inclusion of a magical circus. By comparison, New York was almost dark and oppressive. 'More steampunky, I suppose,' she explains. 'It was also another great canvas on which to make the subtle magical twists.'

There is a lot more magic in the new film, which she has found very liberating. 'You can really push it to extremes.'

Working in concert with the prop making department run by Pierre Bohanna, many of the magical items which populate scenes are built precisely for the occasion.

There are also the multifarious items bought at markets: salvaged lampposts, street furniture, and crystal balls imported from China. 'We get about six months,' she explains, 'which is a generous run, and we went to an amazing amount of French markets in the Paris area. We took trucks, and we bought all this stuff, even before we had a script.'

It was a case of gazing into their own crystal ball and thinking 'that could work' or 'I could paint that'.

It took Pinnock's team five days to dress the half-elf Irma Dugard's sheet-strewn attic on Rue Philippe Lorand, where Credence has come in search of his mother. 'When the actress playing Irma came in, she threw herself against the bed, a bit like a child does when they love a place. She is French, and exclaimed, "This is so French. I just feel this is France."'

Left to right: The elegance of the Ministère des Affaires Magiques de la France was successfully achieved thanks to the grand vision of Stuart Craig and the precision of Pinnock's set decoration team; protective rubber outfits for Newt and Bunty hang on his basement wall; a witch emerges carrying one of the fantastic mousse moulds; *(inset)* though unlikely to be seen on camera, this Scribbulus calendar of Newt's was carefully dressed with paper props that reveal the wizard's life.

FAMILY LEGACIES

A brief lesson in wizard prejudice: at the heart of Grindelwald's worldview is a belief in the supremacy of pureblood wizards, of which the Lestrange dynasty is representative.

However, not all pure families are as pure as they seem. The Lestrange family tree will become a pivotal plot device, stolen from the Records Room at Le Ministère des Affaires Magiques de la France. Once the box is opened, the family's pureblood genealogy will be displayed in three dimensions.

'We designed that to be flat; in the process it has been worked into 3D,' says graphic designer Eduardo Lima.

'From a concept point of view that was interesting,' says Miraphora Mina. 'Jo Rowling said what happens in the dialogue, but we didn't know the whole backstory. Like the Black family tree in Harry Potter, we had to ask her for the actual tree. She ended up only giving us one side of the Lestrange tree, so I had to make up the other side of the tree. It's quite complex. You have to be very careful about how they're all related to each other.'

'They are all, like, married to their cousins,' laughs Lima.

'The tree has almost a Hieronymus Bosch type aesthetic,' says Mina, referring to the fifteenth-century Dutch artist famed for his nightmarish depictions of mankind warped by sin.

She adds: 'I can't wait to see it animated.'

Opposite: Leta prepares to open the box; *Clockwise from top left;* Wand in hand, Kama stands on a monument of one of Leta's ancestors; concept art by Dermot Power and Hattie Story of the elaborate gold Lestrange family records box; Leta sits alone in the Lestrange mausoleum; graphic art by MinaLima of the intricate Lestrange family tree.

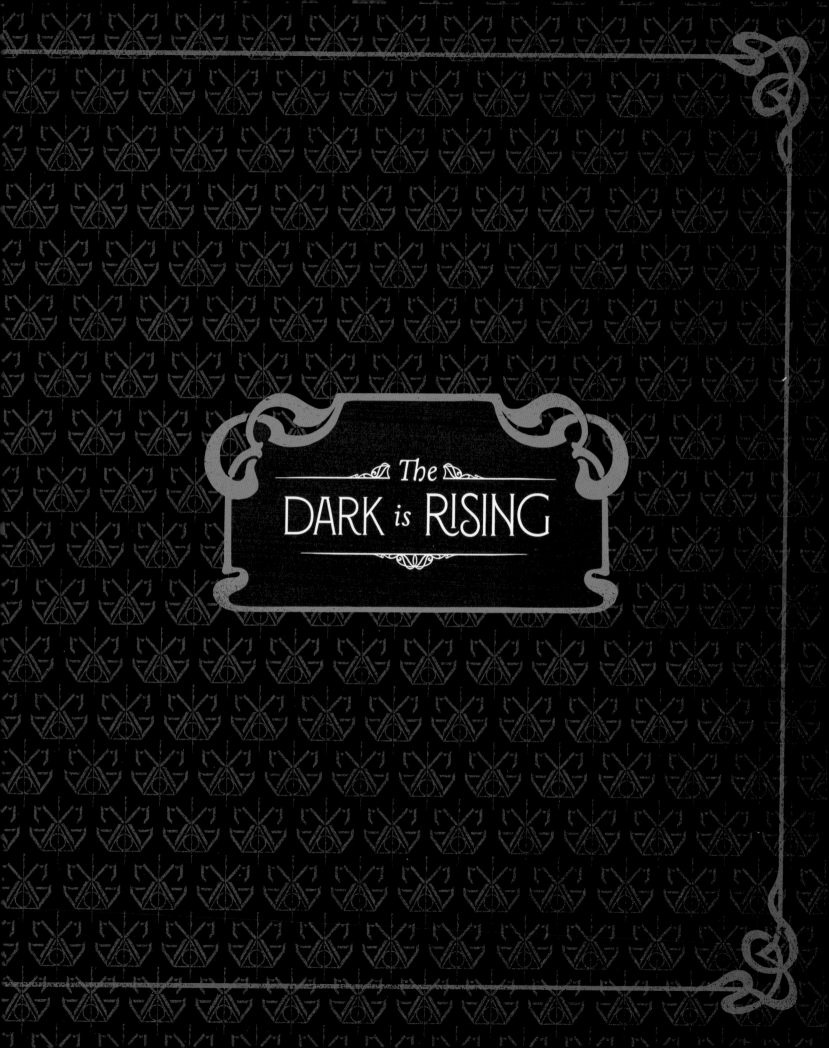

The
DARK is RISING

GELLERT GRINDELWALD

You'll recall that at the dramatic finale of the first film, Colin Farrell's villainous Auror Percival Graves is stripped of his disguise and revealed as none other than Gellert Grindelwald, the most dangerous wizard alive. What's more, he looked exactly like Johnny Depp.

'The whole principle of casting is to go for the finest artists you can,' says director David Yates, 'and Johnny Depp has created two or three of the most iconic characters in popular culture.'

Indeed, that is what is so thrilling about Depp's casting. He is famed for quirky heroes like Edward Scissorhands, Willy Wonka and Captain Jack Sparrow and his menacing turn as a real-life mobster in *Black Mass* has truly revealed a capacity to get under the skin of an absolute blackguard.

Grindelwald is as attractive as he is despicable.

'It's the charisma,' says William Nadylam (Yusuf Kama). 'The character is fascinating because it's Johnny Depp. He's bloody sexy. You know? He looks like a winner.'

This is not a villain who resembles a demon, wrapped in his evil like the corpse-coloured skin of Voldemort. Like a mantra, this is a villain who looks like a rock star.

'This movie deals with the rise of an autocrat, or a man who will be an autocrat if he gets the chance,' explains J.K. Rowling. 'He's a very seductive character and hopefully people will understand why even good-hearted characters are persuaded by him as he begins to gain power.'

Zoë Kravitz says, 'The idea of a villain who is so charismatic and intelligent that you want to believe him. There is something very seductive about someone who's confident and can work a room, and Johnny can certainly do that.'

Remarkably, his cameo on the first film had been kept a secret even from Eddie Redmayne, who was stunned to see the superstar arrive on set with an electric shock of blonde hair and matching moustache, with one unnerving pale-blue eye clashing with one as black as pitch. In the sequel, Grindelwald dresses with a severe Germanic panache: part soldier, part pirate and part dandy, with a long black overcoat, silk waistcoat, black neckerchief, and a pair of knee-high, no-nonsense hunting boots.

'He's a very sophisticated villain in the sense that what he wants to do, really, is to win hearts and minds,' says Yates. 'He wants to convince people that his path is the right path. Voldemort would go around killing people willy-nilly and bludgeoning people with his philosophy. So, you kind of knew who the bad guy was. It was so obvious.'

While he is going to great lengths to ensnare the power of Credence's Obscurus, Grindelwald has also come to Paris to pursue a global agenda.

Grindelwald is obsessed with the idea of seeing wizardkind rise up and take their rightful place in the world. Those he sees as unpolluted by non-wizarding blood. The concern is that he wants to not only dominate non-wizards but also eventually eradicate them entirely.

Which makes him a credible threat to those who believe in love, understanding and curiosity. Yates says, 'Grindelwald makes a case for the path he wants to take us all down, and he pretends he's one of us. He pretends to empathize with us, which makes him probably the most dangerous villain ever.'

His power might one day be superseded by that of Tom Riddle — aka Voldemort — but

Grindelwald's philosophy is potentially more far-reaching as he foments revolution, operating from out of his mountain retreat. 'He's is a compelling speaker,' explains the director, 'and he's playing a longer, cleverer, more dangerous game than the obvious.'

'He has an absolute, one hundred per cent belief system,' says Redmayne, cutting straight to the dark heart of the matter.

It is the force of this obsession that makes him so dangerous. All we know for sure is that his great aunt was wizard historian Bathilda Bagshot.

Grindelwald is a name already notorious to Harry Potter fans. He had another cameo in *Harry Potter and the Deathly Hallows-Part 1* locked up in Azkaban, an old man, withered and possibly mad (in the shape of actor Michael Byrne). We learned that after being expelled from the

Above: Grindelwald tries to convince Queenie.
Opposite (clockwise from top left): Grindelwald surveys his new home; Depp and Colleen Atwood worked together to create Grindelwald's signature look; Grindelwald offers his hand to Leta Lestrange.

Durmstrang Institute, he developed a close friendship with a young Dumbledore (in flashbacks the teenaged Grindelwald was portrayed by Jamie Campbell Bower). Idealistic youths, they sought to liberate wizards from the shackles of the International Statute of Secrecy.

'The story pivots around the relationship between Dumbledore and Grindelwald,' says Yates. 'It's a complicated relationship between these two men who met when they were young, and inspired and encouraged each other, and then fell apart.'

COLLEEN ATWOOD ON GRINDELWALD

Atwood, of course, has dressed Johnny Depp on many occasions. 'We've known each other since *Edward Scissorhands*,' she says, 'and we've done a lot of odd characters together.'

Grindelwald combines a rock star with a dictator. Someone with real charisma, who is able to be seductive, even if he is a dark star. 'We listened to some Marilyn Manson and talked about Grindelwald's Bavarian origins to give it that nod,' she recalls. 'And Johnny explored some the fashions of the thirties, and it all came together. Very black and white to go with his shock of platinum blonde hair, but with dark green elements.'

However, when we are introduced to the wizard, he is in his beige-brown prison garb made from a printed fabric inspired by Japanese fireman. 'Johnny wanted to be covered in cobwebs,' she laughs. 'So we started laying on these tiny, thin threads that look aged and webby.'

GRINDELWALD'S HIDEOUT

THE APARTMENT IN PARIS

Arriving in Paris, Grindelwald and his sinister company of acolytes take over a residence in a well-to-do part of town. The exterior of this apartment was found in the large Paris street layout on the backlot, among the elegant facades and wide boulevards of Haussmann's idealized city.

'Grindelwald's apartment is one of these rather grand places around the Paris Opera,' explains Craig. 'We took lots of photographs from those apartment blocks. We even identified a doorway and stairway in Place des Vosges — bits of location that we could replicate.'

On the first floor is found a grand residence, which they draped in a beautiful silk fabric bought in Paris. 'There isn't any equivalent made here,' says Craig. It also features a large drawing room with a fireplace at both ends.

'It was fun to provide the character detail for a happy and normal French nineteenth-century family that you don't really meet in the flesh,' says set decorator Anna Pinnock. 'But also a challenge to make parts of it creepy and chilling enough to be an appropriate backdrop for Grindelwald's character.'

Another significant challenge was the dramatic unveiling of Grindelwald's banners, which bear the wizard's Art Deco insignia.

Grindelwald is glimpsed through the window of his carriage.

GRINDELWALD'S ACCESSORIES

<table>
<tr><th>THE VIAL</th><th>THE ELDER WAND</th></tr>
</table>

THE VIAL

Around Grindelwald's neck hangs a vial on a chain, in which glows an essence.

'The vial again took an enormous amount of development,' says Bohanna. 'In fact, it has a parallel. A very old, glass perfume vapour-needle runs through the middle of it. It's a beautiful piece. It's amazing — we can spend as much time and effort on something that size as we can on a giant telescope.'

THE ELDER WAND

Grindelwald is also in possession of the Elder Wand — retrieved during his flight from MACUSA. One of the fabled Deathly Hallows, the most powerful of all wands has a Thestral hair at its core. However, in terms of prop design it was a breeze.

'We had made one for the Harry Potter films,' says Bohanna, 'and it really was a beautiful wand. So we just blew the dust off it and got it out again.'

THE SKULL

Together with his dark glamour and platinum blond locks, Grindelwald reveals a collection of magical objects to aid his fiendish conspiracies. A bony vessel, a vial, and a legendary wand: each would require the finest in the Dark Arts from the prop department.

'It took a lot of development,' says special prop designer Pierre Bohanna. 'They always wanted a skull, then maybe an animal's skull, and then having it made out of crystal rather than bone.'

It was only after concept artist Rob Bliss became involved that David Yates settled on a small, yellowish skull with glittering teeth. The macabre receptacle has a pipe with magical vapours also seeping out through the eyes and mouth and a conspicuous hole in the top.

'It's very much a story-driven prop,' says Bohanna. 'In itself it's quite macabre, but in the context of the story they're trying to tell, it's very important.'

Bliss had specialized in what he calls 'a lot of the crazy scary stuff' on the Harry Potter films. After sterling work with Thestrals, Death Eaters and Dementors, he jokes that he ended up being the go-to guy for Goth

Main image: Final skull prop on dressed set, lit from within to demonstrate the magical glow that will be seen in the film. *Inset (from left to right)* The Elder Wand; prop of the sinister skull-pipe complete with Grindelwald's credo, 'For the Greater Good' painted on in German; prop design by Molly Sole of Grindelwald's vial.

stuff: 'It was just like, "Oh, that's scary. Give it to Rob".'

Initially, he had only been tasked with refining pre-existing concepts for the skull. 'The way it was described was, "We've already got a design, and don't change it",' he says. 'So I came in and changed it.'

He was thinking about how they decorated the skulls of church elders and saints in Austrian and Germany in Medieval times. 'As a way of commemorating people there were all these lovely skulls that have been painted with the name of the people and roses and beautiful old Gothic lettering.'

If not quite so decorative, he gave the skull the look of a holy relic that has been preserved and polished.

Then Rowling dropped by the art department. 'I'd been working on this skull design and obviously getting into lots of trouble for having changed the design, and much to my relief she said it was exactly what was inside her head when she was sixteen and had visited an ossuary in Austria. It was as if I had telepathically gone back in time and designed from inside her mind.'

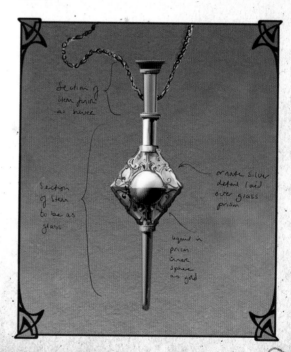

GRINDELWALD'S ACOLYTES

Devoted to their master, a company of seven acolytes will serve Grindelwald while in Paris. They go by the names of Abernathy (the traitor from MACUSA), Nagel, Krall, Carrow, Krafft, MacDuff and Rosier, and are the equivalent of Voldemort's formidable league of Death Eaters in the Harry Potter films.

'I would say we are revolutionaries,' declares Claudius Peters, who plays the scowling Nagel. 'They want to make the world a better place, from their point of view anyway, and they're part of Grindelwald's team in order to do that.'

'They are followers,' agrees Andrew Turner, otherwise known as MacDuff, 'but with a purpose.'

Theirs isn't a blind devotion, but a political belief. Director David Yates was keen for all of Grindelwald's acolytes to be distinct individuals. 'To avoid that sort of homogenized sense of blank-palette baddies,' says Kevin Guthrie, who plays Abernathy. 'We all have to bring our own understanding and belief of what Grindelwald means for our society. There's a real parallel with what might or might not be going on in the world today.'

Poppy Corby-Tuech's menacing Rosier is particularly significant in the wider picture of the wizarding world. Descendants of her line will be among those Death Eaters aiding Voldemort. It

Opposite: Grindelwald and his acolyte, Vinda Rosier, member of a pure-blood family. *Inset:* final prop wands belonging to *(left to right)* Abernathy, Rosier & Krall. *Above, left to right:* Krall (David Sakurai) in Grindelwald's hideout; the traitor Abernathy (Kevin Guthrie) and Rosier.

comes as little surprise that Rosier has made her way up the ranks with Grindelwald.

'Oh, I am Grindelwald's queen woman,' says Corby-Tuech.

While each acolyte will be a distinctive character, there is still a dress code. Anything in dark, muted shades of green, with a dash of red here and there. 'Really classy sort of 1920s stuff,' says Peters.

'I really wanted them to be people,' explains costume designer Colleen Atwood. 'The casting was great because they each had a look: one guy was more military, one was more of a thug, and one was more mysterious. For the two girls, Rosier and Carrow, I went with a kind of masochistic feeling. They were trapped in Grindelwald's web.'

Rosier, in particular, has a very fine witchy variation on haute couture. 'Oh, that was great,' says Atwood. 'I had these pictures of hats from different periods that I liked and I sat with a hat maker and said, "Can you give this a tweak?"'

Her hat manages a miraculous fusion of twenties fashion and pointy witch's hat.

'It looks wonderful on her, as she's such a great looking girl,' says Atwood. 'Then with Carrow's hat, I used as a starting point Carmen Ejogo's hat as Seraphina Picquery in the first film.'

To a witch or a wizard, the actors have been having a ball. On the day they were given their wands, they were like kids in a sweetshop. All their wands have their own unique design, and each actor has developed their own style of casting.

'Mine's kind of just cool,' says Peters, 'just like I'm pointing without any effort.'

'Mine is kind of aggressive,' adds Turner.

'A lot of us have grown up reading the Harry Potter books, and then watching the films, so this has been a surreal experience,' says Corby-Tuech. 'Stepping onto the set and seeing characters like Dumbledore and Nicolas Flamel, that's pretty exciting for a Potter geek.'

What is fascinating about Grindelwald is how little effort it seems to take for the evil wizard to get what he wants.

'He toys with people, being charming and terrifying really,' says Corby-Tuech. 'But he really makes you understand why so many people follow Grindelwald.'

STAGING GRINDELWALD'S RALLY

The grand finale for this second, darker *Fantastic Beasts* film is suitably epic. In a huge set-piece that erupts into furious action and magical effects, Grindelwald attempts to rally the wizards of Paris to his cause in a vast and ancient amphitheatre that lies beneath the Lestrange family mausoleum, which itself lies within the genuine Père Lachaise cemetery in Paris.

Here, Grindelwald will have his moment to play to the crowd, reasoning with them, beseeching them, seducing them. He only wishes for magical folk to come out of hiding and take their rightful place.

Here all the main characters and the many strands of the story will finally tie up: Newt, Tina, Queenie, Jacob, Kama, Theseus, Leta, Credence, and the Maledictus.

THE CEMETERY

The art team took a trip to the real Père Lachaise in the east of the city. The tree-lined graveyard rambles over forty-four hectares, with such luminaries as Oscar Wilde, Frédéric Chopin and Jim Morrison among its many residents. They could see straightaway its attractions to the author. As well as gravestones, this is a necropolis of statues, tombs and mausoleums arranged on twisting paths.

'It is set up on a hill, and has this curving arrangement, and it's almost like there is an amphitheatre of tombs around you,' explains art director Martin Foley. 'We knew that there was going to be some kind of rallying point. There are a lot of underground elements in the

The finale – Grindelwald's rally
in the subterranean amphitheatre.

film because the wizarding world is still underground. That is kind of the point.'

The surface composition of the real cemetery suggested what, in their world, lay beneath — an underground amphitheatre.

'Grindelwald is trying to bring the Paris wizards out of the ground,' says Foley. 'So we felt it was a good setting to put this amphitheatre underneath.'

When it came to the precise location of the Lestrange mausoleum, Craig wanted to inject a specific feel of the more Gothic and overgrown Highgate Cemetery in north London. He had read that Père Lachaise had originally been based on the older London graveyard. In fact, Craig had a specific part of Highgate in mind. 'I'd used Highgate before on another film, and realized that there is a section in the oldest part of cemetery which is very interesting.'

He remembered a circular canyon almost, with doorways to tombs leading off this sunken concourse. 'It is something that is so splendid in its design, I wish I could say I designed it,' he says. 'We actually filmed there as a location, one of the few physical locations that we shot on' (the others being Lacock Abbey and suitable streets of London).

'We had to add some fake gravestones to fit in with the real ones,' recalls graphic designer Eduardo Lima. 'With fake wizard names.'

'It was really spooky being in a real cemetery at night with the crew,' says Foley. Which was exactly the atmosphere they were seeking, until the weather took a turn for the worse. Rob Bliss recalls turning up to show David Yates some

creature designs (finding a moment with the director was a logistical challenge within itself), and it was so dark and rainy that they had to huddle beneath an awning as he held his iPhone torch over the top of his illustrations.

With two more days of shooting still to go, much of it involving a complicated chase through the tombs, they decided to regroup at Warner Bros. Studios Leavesden, and rebuild a sliver of Highgate as a set.

Craig says, 'So, in composite shots from visual effects, those three elements — the deep background shots of Père Lachaise, Highgate as a foreground and a bit of Highgate in the studio — will come together into one big cemetery complex.'

THE MAUSOLEUM

The Lestrange family mausoleum stands taller than any other in the cemetery, and comes decorated with an elaborate array of carvings and sculptures. 'The coffins of deceased Lestranges line the shelves,' explains Craig. 'But going down deeper, down some stairs, you enter the amphitheatre.'

'There are layers to it,' says Foley. 'Like vaults and different types of tombs, before the big reveal is the amphitheatre.'

Originally, there was an elaborate sculpture at the centre of the amphitheatre, a great spire covered with sculpted angels. But as they were blocking out Grindelwald's speech, Yates realized he would rather the character have the stage to himself, and not to keep walking around the pillar. Rather than lose this lavish ornament they moved it up to the mausoleum, where the angels represented Leta's ancestors, and full-sized stone ravens roosted at the top — ravens being the Lestrange family symbol.

All the sculptures are done by hand in clay (for close-ups) or polystyrene (background) using drawings provided by the art department. They are then digitally scanned (for visual effects) and moulded so that the construction team can easily reproduce them.

Left to right: This intricately dressed set recreates Highgate cemetery in the studio; Grindelwald pleads his case; Rosier appears relaxed ahead of Grindelwald's rally; Kama marvels at the size of the mausoleum.

'Dave Hodge, who heads up sculpture, bless him, is always at his wit's end,' says construction manager Paul Hayes. 'We never give him enough time. His team has expanded to sixteen on this show. There were so many variations on the sarcophagi.'

THE AMPHITHEATRE

The venue for Grindelwald's speech had to have what Craig calls a monumental quality. 'It is like a classical Roman amphitheatre with a domed roof, which wasn't built physically,' he says. 'We filled the biggest stage at Leavesden with this set, absolutely filled it.'

Along with Le Ministère des Affaires Magiques de la France, this vast stone arena is another fulsome example of the faith Yates and his filmmakers have in the construction of beautiful, giant interior sets, built to the limits of the stage. The awe in the actors' faces doesn't have to be faked.

'Stuart doesn't do anything by half,' says Foley, 'so when you want an amphitheatre, you get a full 4,000-capacity amphitheatre. We have huge Lestrange ravens. They're like ten-feet high holding up the roof with their wings.'

Working off a 3D concept model, visual effects extended the set adding one of the film's recurring motifs of a vast domed ceiling, supported by that circle of stone ravens. In this case, it was modelled on the Pantheon in Rome — a huge, circular temple that possesses the world's largest, unreinforced dome rising to 142 feet at its zenith.

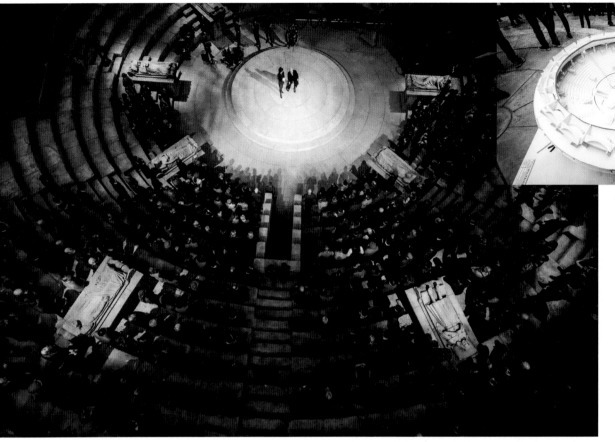

Opposite (clockwise from left): Newt stands unmoved as the audience acclaims Grindelwald; early concept art by Peter Popken depicting Paris being smothered with Grindelwald's black banners; Vinda Rosier presents Grindelwald with his magical skull-pipe. *Left*: Overhead shot reveals the enormous set built to stage Grindelwald's rally; *(inset)* the white card model assembled by Craig's team that the set builders matched, and which was used to plan the visual effects. *Overleaf*: Early concept art by Peter Popken of the aftermath of Grindelwald's rally.

During their research, Craig had found a series of paintings and illustrations of ruined French cemeteries that portrayed both what was above-ground and underground at the same time. 'They kind of break the catacombs open to the sky,' explains concept artist Dermot Power, 'as if to show where it is.'

Yates was so enamoured with their romantic grandeur, he wanted the same effect for the amphitheatre. 'But that didn't make sense,' says Power, 'because that means it is open to the elements.'

The inspired compromise was to have the roof collapsed in one place. Power did a visual of a gaping hole that revealed twelve feet of concrete, then soil and then the trees above. 'So we have light pouring in in a certain way,' he says, 'all very romantic.'

Quite why a chamber of this scale was ever built beneath the cemetery we can only put down to some mysterious wizarding folly, but theme has trumped explanation. 'It is an ancient meeting place for the wizarding fraternity,' supposes Craig. 'The size of it is unexplained, but there is a move in the film through to darker issues, and this very significant confrontation with Grindelwald. You have to feel that this is a worldwide issue. This had to have resonance.'

Compared to New York in the first film it is a stronghold of history. At the very centre is the circular stone dais where Grindelwald makes his entreaties to the crowd, encircled by stone slabs for the tiers of seats on which are carved human figures.

The eyelines alone were dizzyingly complex to map out. Every main actor was present in different parts of the arena, as well as a crowd of extras, all focused on Depp at the centre. Included among their number are many of the background artists in full wizarding gear.

Foley gives a rueful laugh. 'It's one thing for us to build it, and it's a huge set, but to then fill it with the actors and then work out how to shoot it. That was like, "We've done our bit. Good luck!"'

Text by Ian Nathan.

Published in 2018 by
Harper Design
An Imprint of HarperCollins*Publishers*
195 Broadway
New York, NY 10007
Tel: (212) 207-7000
Fax: (855) 746-6023

Distributed throughout the world by
HarperCollins Publishers
195 Broadway
New York, NY 10007

ISBN 978-0-06-285310-3
Library of Congress Cataloguing-in-Publication Data has been applied for.

Project Editor: Chris Smith
Cover design: Simeon Greenaway
Design and layout: Simeon Greenaway
Production Manager: Niccolò De Bianchi

Ian Nathan would like to thank Stuart Craig, Colleen Atwood, Anna Pinnock, Pierre Bohanna, Miraphora Mina, Eduardo Lima, and Dermot Power.

HarperCollins would like to thank Victoria Selover, Emma Whittard, Mickey Stern, Jill Benscoter, Katie MacKay, Katie Khan, and Melanie Swartz.

Printed and bound in Spain
First Printing, 2018